Anonymous

Manual of the Common Council of the City of Buffalo, 1897

Anonymous

Manual of the Common Council of the City of Buffalo, 1897

ISBN/EAN: 9783337301521

Printed in Europe, USA, Canada, Australia, Japan

Cover: Foto ©Suzi / pixelio.de

More available books at **www.hansebooks.com**

MANUAL————

OF THE

COMMON COUNCIL

CONTAINING

A SKETCH OF BUFFALO,

Facts and Figures on Various Subjects, a List of
Members of the BOARD of ALDERMEN,
COUNCILMEN and COMMON COUNCIL,
constituting the Legislative
Branches of

THE CITY GOVERNMENT,

Together with a Full and Corrected
Statement of all Appointments
and the Salaries of

MUNICIPAL OFFICERS,

Details and Duties of Public Departments,
Vote Required on Various Measures,
and full Data Relative to
Public Affairs for
the Year

1897.

THE WENBORNE-SUMNER COMPANY,
PRINTERS AND BOOKMAKERS,
61-69 CARROLL ST., BUFFALO, N. Y.

CITY CLERK'S OFFICE,

City and County Hall,
BUFFALO, N. Y.

TO WHOM IT MAY CONCERN:

I Hereby Certify, *That at a Session of the Board of Aldermen of the City of Buffalo, held in the City and County Hall on the 1st day of February, A. D. 1897, a resolution was adopted, of which the following is a true copy:*

Alderman Smither, from the Committee on Finance, reported as follows:

Your Committee on Finance, to whom was referred, under date of January 11, communication from Mark S. Hubbell, City Clerk, asking for authority as to the number of copies of the City Manual to be issued for the year 1897, respectfully recommend:

That the number of said Manuals to be issued be determined to be 10,000, of which number 1,000 to be bound in Morocco, and the remainder in the ordinary style of binding, as heretofore.

Adopted.

And that at a Session of the Board of Councilmen of the City of Buffalo, held in the City and County Hall, on the 3d day of February, A. D. 1897, the action of the Board of Aldermen in passing said resolution was duly concurred in.

And I further certify that said resolution was submitted to his Honor, the Mayor of said City of Buffalo, by whom the same was approved on the 15th day of February, 1897.

ATTEST:

MARK S. HUBBELL, City Clerk.

CITY HALL DIRECTORY.

General Office Hours in All Municipal Offices, 8:30 a. m. to 4:30 p. m., fixed by ordinance.

County Offices fixed by Heads of the Departments individually.

FIRST FLOOR.

Room 1...............Board of Public Works.
      2....................City Treasurer.
      3........................Comptroller.
      4.........................City Clerk.
      5...............Park Commissioners.
      6. Coroners and "Press" Headquarters.
      7.........Superintendent of Streets.
      8...........................Sheriff.
      9...................County Clerk.
      10........................Surrogate.
      11.................County Treasurer.

SECOND FLOOR.

Room 12........................Mayor.
      13................Chief Engineer.
      14...........Supreme Court, Part 3.

CITY HALL DIRECTORY—*Continued.*
SECOND FLOOR,

Room 15. . . . . Assessors.
"   16. . . . . District Attorney.
"   17. .Grand Jury.
"   18. . . . . Superior Court Chambers.
"   19. . . . . .Commissioner of Jurors.
"   20. . . . . County Judge.
"   21. . . . . .County Court.
"   22. . . . . .Supreme Court, Part 1.
"   23. . . . . .Law Library.
"   24. .Judges' Private Consulting Room.
"   25. . . . . Supreme Court Chambers.
"   26. . . . . . .Supreme Court, Special Term.
"   27 . . . . Superior Court Records.

THIRD FLOOR.

Room 28.   . . .Board of Councilmen.
"   29.   . .Board of Aldermen.
"   30.   . . Court Juries.
"   31.   Corporation Counsel.
"   32. . . . . .Supreme Court, Equity Term.
"   33. . .   . . .Justices.
"   34. .   . .Supreme Court, Part 2.
"   35.   Supervisors.
"   36.   .Clerk to Supervisors.
"   37.   . .County Auditor.

ANCIENT HISTORY OF BUFFALO.

ONE HUNDRED YEARS ago the site of the City of Buffalo was a small trading post, or trappers' settlement. In 1795 one Baron La Rochefoucault Liancourt remarked in memoirs of this, then primeval, region, that, " at the post on Lake Erie there is a small collection of four or five houses."

But the little settlement had a future. By the year 1800 the Holland Land Company had acquired much of the site of the present great city by purchase, and in preparing to lay it out in town and village lots, had christened it "New Amsterdam," a name which mercifully fell from it like the cocoon from the moth, before its godfather, the late Joseph Ellicott, nicknamed "The Bay Window," was gathered to his fathers in a better and less divisible land. The surveys were completed in 1804, and the first lot, containing half an acre, was sold for $135. The young village throve, and was duly incorporated April 2, 1813, and on December 30, the same year, was destroyed by British troops and their Indian allies, who crossed the river at Black Rock on their errand of destruction. But two houses escaped the flames, and they served as a nucleus around which grew up a colony, which in 1832 was officially recognized as a city, and duly incorporated. Thenceforward it had a healthy, but not a phenomenal growth, until about the year 1870, when it began to roll up cumulatively astonishing additions to its population, and to give evidence of becoming some day one of the greatest commercial and manufacturing cities in the civilized world. That expectation has already been realized. Its growth between 1880 and 1890 was like compounding interest on money, and was in every way phenomenal, and the development has continued until to-day, when it is generally conceded that Buffalo affords the best field for speculative enterprises and for manufacturing undertakings of any of the cities of its size in the world. The latter statement being particularly verified by the fact that Niagara Falls is now actually furnishing the motive power for the street railways of Buffalo, will be at the service of all manufacturers within six months from March 1, 1897, and will give Buffalo the best and cheapest power in the world, unobtainable anywhere else on earth.

THE MOST CENTRAL SHIPPING POINT IN THE COUNTRY.

THE MANUAL OF 1896.

ONE of the greatest military geniuses of the world, on the burning sands of Egypt, exclaimed to his cohorts: "Soldiers, from yonder pyramids forty centuries look down upon you," and so it may be said of the Buffalo of to-day—that upon her progress, growth and achievement are fixed the eager eyes of the scientific and financial Genii of this world. It is one of the most rapidly growing cities in the universe. It has swept to the front, in the procession of cities, with giant strides, from a place far in the rear, and through its enterprise has been achieved the greatest miracle of science—the subjection of the power of the Falls of Niagara to the uses of mankind, the story of which will be told later in these pages.

When the Manual of 1896 was put forth it opened wider the eyes of those who received it to the great advantages of Buffalo. They were claims which could not be ignored, and they shouldered their way to the front, in comparison with the claims of other cities to attention, like Titans striding through an army of pigmies, for they showed among other things that the lake tonnage of this city crowds closely that of Liverpool, and prove by actual figures that Buffalo is the fourth greatest port of entry and clearance on the globe.

The Manual of 1896 told the story of noble work accomplished, of splendid achievements consummated, and of greater undertakings and expectations.

This Manual of 1897 tells the story of how those expectations were realized, and offers to thousands who are eagerly seeking such matter an opportunity to grasp, in condensed form, a succinct story of development.

Whenever great deeds are accomplished there are those who snarl thereat ; envy, like death, loves a shining mark, and at the heels of the mastiff of progress snarl ever the yelping kennels of disappointed ambition and baffled hope. Empires are like states, states like cities, cities like villages, and villages like individuals; because the empire, the state, the city and the village are ruled by coteries of personalities, reproducing their own likenesses and mirroring their own vices, as well as their virtues; so cities, falling behind in the procession of progress are like envious singers even in church choirs, who, while chanting hosannas to the Almighty, deprecate the abilities of their betters.

Strange that prosperity, the fruit of endeavor, incited by honorable ambition, should breed, instead of emulation, envy and abuse! From Rochester and Cleveland newspapers came vituperation, and from Detroit silence, while greater cities, cast in more splendid molds and governed by more noble minds, through their newspapers, hailed the growth of the greatest inland lake city in the United States, next to Chicago, with acclamation and praise; and from the Golden Gate of San Francisco came those generous plaudits from the Examiner and Chronicle of that city which are born only in municipalities and individuals from an assurance of their own greatness. Philadelphia, New York, Baltimore, St. Louis, all paid generous tribute to the facts set forth in the book in question, and so Buffalo, having secured the approval of the great, can well afford to smilingly pursue the tenor of its way to that position of proud pre-eminence foretold by Nikola Tesla on an occasion to be referred to later on, which shall stamp it as the greatest inland city in the world.

EDGAR B. JEWETT,
Mayor.

THE BUFFALO OF TO-DAY.

Being a Chapter upon Municipal Themes, and
Narrating Briefly the Accomplishment
of Great Achievements.

BUFFALO is already the greatest railroad
center in the United States, and includes more trackage than New York,
Chicago or St. Louis.

Twenty-six great railroad corporations
operate their roads through Buffalo; and 250
or more passenger trains enter and leave the
city every day.

Every mile of trackage is a crystallization,
into iron and steel, of human faith, for men
do not spend money heedlessly, nor do soulless
corporations lay tracks without having duly
measured and estimated the returns from their
investment.

Buffalo had 660 miles of railway trackage in
actual operation in 1896, and the two years
which have passed have added many miles to
that great aggregate, an accurate statement of
which is rather the work of the statistician
than the generalizer. The railroads own

nearly 4,000 acres of land within the city
limits, and many of them have Buffalo as
their terminal point, connecting here with
trunk lines for the West or East. It is here
that the ore, mined in the region about Lake
Superior and in the western country, passes on
its way to the foundries and smelting works;
and the coal products of Pennsylvania, west-
ward bound, pass the western cargoes going
East.

Buffalo is an exchange point for more trades
and traffic than any other city in the world,
and it may be stated as a demonstrable fact
that its average yearly business in live stock
alone amounts to over 7,600,000 head;
and it is estimated that 7,250,000 net
tons of coal come to Buffalo as an exchange
and distributing point every year. It may
thus be justly regarded as a central and headquarters point for the coal, the lumber, live
stock and railroad interests of the country.
It is the largest sheep and horse market in
the world.

RAPID INTER-URBAN TRANSIT.

There are 150 miles of street railway in the
City of Buffalo, and it has been promised
that 30 miles more, opening new territory,
will be built this year by a ''new'' company.

THE MOST CENTRAL SHIPPING POINT IN THE COUNTRY.

The Buffalo Railway Company, which operates all Buffalo surface railways except the Niagara Falls line, which runs over its tracks in the city limits, is composed of capitalists in Buffalo, Philadelphia, New York and other leading cities, whose names are themselves potent factors in the world of finance.

This company operates about 550 cars, employs between 1,800 and 2,000 men, paying, it is said, as high wages as are paid street railway employes anywhere in the country.

There is not now a single street car drawn by horses within the 42 square miles of Buffalo. The most perfect transfer system in the world is used here. A single fare of five cents is charged, carrying with it the privilege of transferring in any one continuous direction, over any number of lines, a privilege which may be, and often is taken advantage of, so that a passenger with five cents can travel between ten and twelve miles, from one city line to the other. Cars are heated by electricity, represent a safe and satisfactory average of rapid transit, run on most lines all night, and on all lines at very frequent intervals.

Accidents are infrequent, and the front of every car is equipped with a life-saving device, consisting of an iron frame, filled in with rope netting, which has already many times demonstrated its usefulness.

The father of the Buffalo street railway system was Stephen Van Rensselaer Watson, and the family name of that public spirited and esteemed citizen has become synonymous with excellence in street railroad circles. The roads, when they were re-organized by the present syndicate, some years ago, recognized this by electing Henry M. Watson, formerly of Gov. Cornell's staff, and a prominent and energetic Buffalonian, to a position of high trust in its management. To his rare executive ability and to his wisdom in the choice of his subordinates is due the thanks of the community for the excellent service it now enjoys. He spared no expense in importing from other cities capable assistants who could be depended upon to carry out his ideas, and the results of his superior management are abundantly manifest.

The gross earnings of the Buffalo Railway Co., for the quarter ending December 3, 1896, as reported by the Company, were $337,900 ; net earnings, $170,702 ; other income, $6,000 ; fixed charges, $108,024 ; net income, $68,677 ; same quarter of last year, net income, $78,305.

—

THE MOST CENTRAL SHIPPING POINT IN THE COUNTRY.

The percentage paid the city, last year, on
the company's gross receipts was $45,613.74,
as against $39,613.07 in 1895.

This company carried in 1896, 53,303,789
passengers as against 44,964,609 in 1895, and
this remarkable showing of transportation
afforded is made more remarkable by the fact
that there are at least 50,000, and by many
competent judges estimated 60,000, bicycles
in the City of Buffalo, of which probably
two-thirds are used as practical vehicles of
transportation from the homes of the owners
to their offices during at least eight months
of the year, thus seriously cutting into the
business and income of the street railway
companies.

A new company, christened the Buffalo
Traction Company, and promising "competition," obtained a franchise from the Common
Council in 1896, and under this franchise it is
expected some 30 miles of track will be laid
this year.

TO NIAGARA FALLS BY TROLLEY.

Two years ago, the Buffalo & Niagara Falls
Electric Railway sprang into existence, backed
by large capital in the control of able and far-
seeing business men. They built a throughly
ballasted railroad, capable of carrying on its

rails any steam railroad train, from Buffalo
to Niagara Falls, and despite the prophecies of
those who believed the enterprise would not
pay, this excellent line, summer and winter,
is operated at a big margin of profit. Its cars
are arranged like the steam railway coaches,
having observation and smoking apartments,
and are heated and lighted by electricity. A
trip to the Falls, over this line, gives the
traveler an idea of the territory lying between
here and the great cataract, and the manifest
destiny of all this tract of land is to, one day,
form a continuous built-up city connecting
Buffalo and Niagara Falls.

It has been justly alleged of Buffalo that its
eminence as a manufacturing city is assured,
and it has already been called with much
reasonable analogy "The Manchester of the
New World," but the original Manchester has
no such bright future ahead of it as its name-
sake. The latter, already one of the greatest
industrial cities of the country, manufactures
among other important commercial products,
mammoth steel and iron steamships, marine
boilers and engines, locomotives, Wagner
palace cars, agricultural implements, milling
machinery, flour, wall paper, iron bridge
work, cast iron pipe, brick, lithographic

THE MOST CENTRAL SHIPPING POINT IN THE COUNTRY.

work, soap, starch, printing ink, patent medi-
cines, fertilizers, illuminating and lubricating
oils, and has scale works, smelting works and
foundries among its industries.

WORKING FOR UNCLE SAM.

A case in point : When the national government wanted steel barbettes made for its
splendid cruisers, it had to come to Buffalo as
the only city in the country possessing engineering facilities to supply its wants. These
are but a few Buffalo industries incidentally
mentioned, out of the many. All the sunny
grain sheaves of the prairie, all the shining
pyrites of the mines, all the varied products
of the Northwest, grow and are developed,
garnered, mined or harvested to some day
find their way to this city, either here to be
converted to the uses of mankind, to pass
through here to the eastern markets, or hence
to find their way by ship-board to Europe.
The destiny of at least some out of every herd
of cattle in every "round-up" by western
cowboys is to pass through Buffalo on the
hoof or in refrigerator cars as merchantable
commodities. A writer in the New York
Tribune stated two years ago, reviewing the
situation, that he saw no reason why Buffalo,
with its tremendous natural advantages and

resources, should not one day be the metropolis of America. And what mammoth strides have been made since then. And what still more splendid prophecies as to her future have since been made by lips almost inspired and by men who weigh with careful exactitude the consequences of each word they utter.

And while the railroads and steamboats have, almost literally, on the pilots of their engines and the prows of their great steel propellers, pushed Buffalo up to greatness, they have at the same time made null the prophecy of the croakers, who, with eyes turned constantly upon the past, averred that railroad development meant death to the Lake and Canal carrying trade : the Lake interests grew greater and the amounts invested in floating property more enormous. The dawn of 1896 saw the launching of Leviathans of steel, rivalling in tonnage capacity, in size and beauty, the "gray-hounds" of the seas ; and in line with the State improvement of the Erie Canal to meet an increased volume of commerce, the federal authorities have awakened to the fact that this is a city the development of which is not to be arrested and whose demands for public expenditure are based upon the soundest public polity.

THE MOST CENTRAL SHIPPING POINT IN THE COUNTRY.

A FOUR-MILLION DOLLAR BREAKWATER.

In January, 1896, the Congressional Committee on Rivers and Harbors, listened for nearly two hours to arguments made before its members by a large delegation of Buffalonians, and finally reported to the Congress of the United States a bill, recommending the expenditure, in this city, for the improvement of its breakwater facilities, upon the continuous contract plan, of $4,000,000, in money. The contract for this work has now been signed, and with the breaking of the winter the labors thereon will be at once begun and steadily prosecuted until completion.

But this is slow work, to be accomplished in defiance of winds and angry waters, and time must pass before this end is reached.

True, Grover Cleveland's last official act was to veto the appropriation bill providing for the completion of the new Post Office, and the harbor improvement of Buffalo, but a Republican Congress will re-enact the bill and a Republican President will sign it, and the Post Office building will be finished and the harbor improvements carried to completion.

When that great public work is consummated Buffalo will have one of the noblest and one of the largest harbors in the world, and there will spring from this appropriation of Congress the inception of a splendid system of municipal dockage, plans for which have already been conceived and only await the opportunity to be put into active execution. From the old light-house at the mouth of the inner harbor to a point four miles toward the south shore of Lake Erie, as the crow flies, is a noble stretch of water washing the beach, where Lake Erie curves to turn southward. This has been but partially protected by a mile and a quarter of breakwater, built by the United States government some years ago and never perfectly completed.

The system of breakwaters which the government has undertaken to construct, will consist of three substantial structures, echeloned one after the other and as in a procession, except that the ends of each, starting from the end of the present breakwater will overlap each other, with a distance of half a mile between each end. This will afford perfect protection against the driving waves, allowing none of them to enter directly into the space enclosed, but at the same time giving the water from the Lake an easy flow into the harbor.

From the shore, sheltered by these mammoth dikes, the docks of Buffalo, which may rival the famous docks of Liverpool, will be built, and in the space enclosed could be harbored the navies of the world.

THE LARGEST OFFICE BUILDING IN THE WORLD.

A word in passing, concerning Ellicott Square. This superb structure occupies one of the largest blocks on Main street, extending through to Washington street, and bounded on the north by South Division street, and on the south by Swan street; it is ten stories high, and contains 447,000 square feet of floor space; the decorations are in Italian marble, marble mosaic and ornamental iron; the finish is quarter-sawed red oak. The building is heated by the overhead steam system; it contains 40 stores, 16 banking offices and counting rooms, and 600 offices; it is 144 feet high, has 15 hydraulic passenger elevators, of the Otis pattern; its frame is of steel, weighing 5,550 tons; the exterior construction is of pressed brick and terra cotta, and the foundation of steel and concrete, extending 19 feet below grade. The cost of the site and building was about $3,350,000, and the first and second mortgage bonds thereon were bought by Kidder, Peabody & Co., of Boston. As the offices are largely occupied by members of the legal profession,

a first-rate law library is one of the con-
veniences in this great building. The tenants
housed therein constitute a world in themselves, and those working beneath its roof
would easily equal the population of many a
little city. It is interesting to note regarding this great structure, that, from the
time the first pick was put on the roof of one
of the old buildings, on Main street, preliminary to clearing the ground for excavation,
until the last finishing touch was added to
the new building, was just one year.

THE MIGHTY VOICE OF LABOR.

It was stated before a Common Council Committee, within a few weeks, by a leader of
labor organizations and one who ought to
know whereof he spoke, that 26,000 votes were
cast in Buffalo, on Nov. 3, by members of
labor organizations, showing that one-third of
Buffalo's voting population belongs to the
brawny hordes of honest toil, for 65,692 was
the total number of votes cast, in this city, on
that date. And while perfectly organized for
self-protection, and, in instances, for aggres-
sion, this great army of organized toilers has,
as a rule, had judicious leaders, who politely
asked before they demanded, and who have
usually, through considerate and conservative

THE MOST CENTRAL SHIPPING POINT IN THE COUNTRY.

efforts, secured fair play for their followers without trenching or imposing upon the rights of the employers. The few great strikes which Buffalo has had have been railroad strikes, incited from without and carried forward by the indefatigable efforts of non-resident "organizers," which is mentioned to show that Buffalo's wage-workers are not of the class that strike and agitate willfully or habitually.

WAGE-WORKERS OWN THEIR HOMES.

And there is a reason for this, which lies in the fact that Buffalo, through the healthful influence of its savings and loan associations, movements which began here nearly a quarter of a century ago and have been growing ever since, is a city of homes; and through these associations the workingman, by paying a very small amount per week, is enabled to purchase and finally totally acquire a roof over his head and a habitation for his family, which he can call his own. Strikes injure property interests, and property owners do not like strikes, for they increase taxation; and the Buffalo workingman, owning his own home and being to that extend a landed proprietor opposes anything that will tend in the direction of curtailing the opportunities of labor, disturbing the conditions of trade and increasing the amount to be raised by taxation.

WE AND OUR NEIGHBORS.

It is but a question of a few months before Tonawanda will be a city ward, and take its rightful place as a section of Greater Buffalo.

A bill is at this writing before the Legislature to take into the city limits Buffalo's near neighbor on the north ; this will include Kenmore, a prosperous little settlement just across the present city line, and through which runs the brick-paved boulevard, 100 feet wide, which connects the city with the town. Annexation will add to the population of Buffalo about 12,000 people, and will be the first extension of the city limits accomplished in over 40 years. The result should be mutually satisfactory, and so far as the rate-payers in Tonawanda are concerned it will materially lighten their burden of taxation, while giving them the advantage of city life. Buffalo's tax rate is materially less than Tonawanda's per 1,000 of valuation. The benefit to the townsmen of annexation is more easily demonstrable than the benefit to the citizens.

THE MOST CENTRAL SHIPPING POINT IN THE COUNTRY.

But Buffalo and Tonawanda are already one except in name. A boy in the second-story window of the last house in Buffalo could send a projectile, which, aimed properly, would break a windowpane in the nearest house in Tonawanda. Taking their business together, these places constitute the largest lumber trade center in the world.

BANKING CAPITAL LARGELY INCREASED.

Eighteen banks of deposit and discount, five savings banks and two trust companies are doing business in Buffalo. The total capital represented amounts to $5,550,000; the total surplus and undivided profits is $4,251,570; and the total deposits aggregate $34,987,360, making the total resources $45,464,234. These figures were obtained from officers of the Buffalo Clearing House. They were compiled from the December, 1896, statement of 18 discount banks, and January, 1897, statement of two trust companies.

The Clearing House was established on April 1, 1889, and during the time that has since elapsed there has been a marked increase in the number of banks, in the amount of resources and in the general banking business. When the Clearing House was established there were but 13 banks in the city with a total capital of $3,650,000; surplus and undivided profits $2,500,000; deposits $22,400,-000; and total resources $28,550,000. During the year 1896 the Clearing House showed clearings amounting to $219,400,646, and balances of $38,635,899.

NATURAL GAS FOR FUEL.

Natural gas, since 1886, has been a standard article of fuel; it averages favorably, for household use, with coal, in cost, and is an avoidance of dirt and an enormous saving of labor to the householders. There are over 100 miles of pipe laid through the City, by which this modern convenience is conveyed. It is piped here from various points in Pennsylvan and Canada, new wells being constantly added to the central supply, so that the predicted exhaustion of this unequalled fuel will hardly come to pass in this day and generation.

LIBERAL PUBLIC POLICY.

The municipal government is at all times a liberal one. It fosters enterprise and encourages the advent of a stranger. Its unwritten policy has always been founded upon the lines indicated by the great statesman who wrote : "That governs best which governs least". No income is derived by the municipality from many lines of industry heavily taxed in other places. Unreasonable sumptuary laws are not enforced by the police authorities, and such regulations alone are operative as secure paternally the greatest good to the greatest number.

THE CITY GOVERNMENT.

The city works under a Revised Charter, which became a law in 1892. It was framed by a committee of citizens representing the best of Buffalo's business, social and political life. This model instrument provides for a Board of Aldermen, comprised of 25 representatives, one from each of the 25 wards (as the city grows and adds wards to its population each will be entitled to a representative to take his place in the Board). This body originates all legislation in the city government. All action taken thereby is inoperative unless approved by the Board of Councilmen, made up of nine men elected on a general ticket. This body does not originate legislation, but is distinctively a board of review, and above and beyond it stands the Chief Executive, the Mayor. Matters passing both boards and reaching him may be defeated at his hands by the interposition of a veto. This, however, may be over-ridden by 18 votes of the "Lower House," or Board of Aldermen, and seven votes of the "Upper house," or Board of Councilmen, when it becomes operative, notwithstanding the opposition of His Honor, the Mayor.

The new Constitution of the State of New York, framed by the Constitution Convention of 1894, did away with the admixture of State, national and local politics, by so amending the Charter of the city that municipal officers must be chosen at separate elections, and providing for a two-year term of service of Aldermen after the inauguration of the new system so framed should have been completed. Under this it became necessary in 1894 to elect all Aldermen for three-year terms; Aldermen elected in 1895 will serve two years, and an entirely new board will be elected in 1897, taking office on January 1, 1898, to serve two years each.

The Legislature amended the Charter so as to provide for the election of three Councilmen in 1895 to serve for four years, and it was also enacted "that six Councilmen shall be elected in 1897, and they shall meet before the end of the year, at a time and place to be designated by the Mayor, and determine by lot, two of their number to hold office for two years, and shall certify in writing to the City Clerk their determination. The term of office of the Councilmen elected in 1897, and so certified, shall be two years and the others shall be four years." At the annual election held in odd numbered years thereafter "it is provided there shall be elected alternately five and four Councilmen for the term of four years," and the terms of other city officers also expire with the end of the odd-numbered years, successors to be elected the preceding fall.

And thus the machinery of the new constitution has been perfected and set in motion so that all city offices to become vacant will be filled by election in odd numbered years, no municipal election occurring hereafter at the same time as elections for State or other offices.

CAREFUL CONTROL OF PUBLIC MONEY.

The fiscal affairs of the city are governed and administered by a Comptroller and City Treasurer. No General Fund indebtedness, however, can be incurred without a two-thirds vote in both legislative bodies and the approval

of His Honor, the Mayor. Buffalo's municipal debt is small as compared with other
cities, and its tax rate low in comparison with
its assessed valuation. Facts and figures will
be found tersely stated upon another page,
showing in a brief and available form the
advantages of Buffalo in these and other re-
gards from many points of view.

TEACHING THE YOUNG IDEA.

Buffalo has a most efficient system of public
instruction. It has 60 public schools, which include two high schools, one on the east, the
other on the west side of the city, with a total
enrollment for the year 1896 of 52,157 pupils, an
increase of 5,492 over the previous year, the
largest increase ever recorded, an indication
that the public schools are growing in favor
and have the confidence of the community. The
number of children attending all other schools
is 19,082, making a total school registration
of 71,239. The attendance at the Buffalo High
School has increased from 300 pupils in 1883
to 2,000 in 1896.

Through the grades of the grammar schools
and the High School curriculum the child
of the poorest parents may successfully
progress until he or she is in every way

equipped to enter the freshman class of any of the great universities of the country. Graduates from the Buffalo High school have successfully prosecuted courses at Heidelburg and Oxford, and found it easy to compete with pupils turned out as finished from any of the famous schools of the old world.

Within the last few years, a better and more systematic course of training in civil government has been introduced into the schools. In the primary grades, without sacrifice of thoroughness in "the three R's," preliminary instruction in literature and science is given to the children in attractive form, thus teaching them as early as possible to recognize the beautiful in literature and to know something at least of the living, growing world as it really is.

The appointment of a woman three years ago to supervise the work done in the primary grades proved such a success that a man has recently been appointed to do similar work in the grammar grades. An improvement of method and a greater unity of purpose among the teachers is the result.

MANUAL TRAINING AND SEWING.

Among the recent improvements in the public schools is the introduction of manual

training. Two fully equipped manual training rooms are in operation, one at No. 31,
a representative east side school, and the other
at No. 51 on the west side, tending to the
same end but at a less cost. Sloyd or simple
knife work has been introduced into some
other schools, and always with satisfactory results. Sewing as a part of the regular school
course is no longer an experiment, and sewing
classes have been organized in all the largest
schools of the city under the instruction of
four competent teachers. The city pays 10
kindergartners, who work under the auspices
of the free kindergarten association.

With the co-operation of factory inspectors
and the health department, more has been done
to break up truancy than ever before. Buffalo
is to have its long talked of Truant School.
An unoccupied school house on Dole street has
been fitted up and will be ready for use this
year. This school for truants is needed to
give backbone to the compulsory education
system.

Another school established under the city is
the training school for teachers, which holds
its sessions in public school No. 10. It has
40 pupils and two instructors. Miss Katherine
Hurlburt, the principal, is a woman of large

and varied experience in the work of training young teachers; for the betterment of the schools it is one of the most important movements in the recent educational history of the city.

FREE SCHOOL BOOKS.

The system of free school books was introduced into the Buffalo schools three years ago. Last year for the first time books were furnished to the night schools. The total cost of books for the school department for 1896 was $29,689.39. Of the books purchased 2,637 were for the High school, and 59,857 for the other schools. There were in addition 50,540 drawing and writing books, 8,000 musical readers, and 200 charts. The draft upon the free school book system was especially heavy this year because of the enactment of the temperance instruction law, thus making it obligatory on the city to provide the schools with physiologies containing the requisite number of pages devoted to the effects of alcohol and narcotics. The estimated cost of the free school system book this coming year is $25,000. A table giving the cost per pupil of maintaining this system in different cities where it has been introduced indicates that it has been managed in Buffalo with unusual care and economy. Yet pupils were never so well provided with books. School authorities in many cities have asked explanation of Buffalo's method of conducting the system. Since the introduction of the free school book system there has been a steady decrease in the cost per pupil, which was 66 cents in 1893 and '94, 63 cents in '94 and '95, and 57 cents in '95 and '96.

A Board of School Examiners is a part of the public school system, and candidates for teachers have to pass an examination before this body of censors. Their work has been highly satisfactory and the personnel of the Boards will be found elsewhere in these pages.

A TEACHERS' UNION.

The Buffalo Women Teachers' Association is the only body of teachers in the world that owns its own real estate. It is composed of 600 women teachers, who meet to discuss educational work and methods with the aim of rendering better and more efficient work of the individual teacher. Two years ago this body of women accumulated $500, with which sum they made their first payment on the Chapter House, their present home. Today the property with its furnishings is valued at

BUFFALO HISTORICAL SOCIETY BUILDING.

$16,000, and the debt on it has been reduced to
$6,500, which the teachers are working hard
to pay off. Any mention of the Women
Teachers' Association would be incomplete
without reference to the work of Dr. Ida C.
Bender, who was instrumental in forming the
association, and who has been its president
for the past seven years. To her untiring
efforts and enthusiasm much of the present
success is due.

THE PUBLIC HISTORICAL SOCIETY.

During February, 1897, the Common Council
of the city accepted an offer from the Buffalo
Historical Society, for many years a prominent and valuable Buffalo institution, conducted and operated by private capital, to turn
over its property, including rare collections of
local and general interest, upon the city
agreeing to pay $25,000 into the building
fund of the society and secure for it a site in
the Buffalo Park, near the main driveway and
accessible by the Forest and Elmwood Avenue
cars. This arrangement was consummated
through the energy of Mr. Andrew Langdon,
President of the Society, who took upon his
own shoulders the raising of $35,000 to
make up the deficiency of the sum total of

$100,000, which it is estimated the new building will cost. The plans shown provide for a noble, two story, stone structure, not unlike, in its general style of architecture, that of the Laflin Memorial Building in Lincoln Park, Chicago. Accommodations for the Park Patrol corps will be provided in the basement.

A NOBLE NEW PUBLIC BUILDING.

The main floor will be sky-lighted from above, and comprise in its interior arrangements a great hall, running the entire length of the building and extending to the roof, alcoves opening upon it from either side. An idea of the general value of the collections of this institution may be afforded from the statement that the accessions to its shelves during the past year include 298 volumes, 694 pamphlets, making a total library of 9,121 volumes and 7,379 pamphlets. The treasures of the society include the Dr. John C. Lord collection of relics and curios, the Adrian R. Root collection of war relics, Dr. Joseph C. Green's collection of 300 originals and casts of Egyptian, Syrian and Assyrian antiquities, the Jonathan Scoville collection of Indian relics, Dr. Frank H. Green's collection of coins, medals and medallions. The news paper collection is the most complete in the city and contains files from the beginning of the century. A practically useful compilation is the society's record of marriages and deaths from 1811 up to the time of the establishment of the bureau of vital statistics in 1878, as it is the only place in Buffalo where these old archives may be consulted.

The society numbers 13 honorary members; 135 life members, who have paid $50 each; life membership was raised some time ago to $100. There are 300 resident members, who pay $5 yearly, and 125 corresponding members. All these questions of membership will be passed upon by the joint committee of members of the society and the city in the re-adjustment of its affairs. The collections of the Historical Society rank in value with the first in the country. During the past three years an average of 29,000 people have visited the society rooms. Every year a course of free lectures on local history and topics of the times is given under the auspices of the society. Millard Fillmore was its founder and first president.

THE NEW CITY HALL AS PROPOSED.

The city boasts the handsomest and best conducted City and County building in the

United States.   It was first occupied in March,
1876, and was constructed "on honor," at a
total cost of $1,400,000.   The building is of
granite, and is ornamented by a tower containing an illuminated electric clock, and at
the corners thereof are four statues symboliz-
ing factors in Buffalo's progress.   The hall is
three stories in height, with paved and
vaulted basement, and in it are nearly all the
City and County offices and Courts.   The
Common Council Chamber is very handsome
and commodious.   An Annex or Municipal
Building was erected on Delaware Avenue,
opposite the City Hall, during the year 1889,
to accommodate the Municipal Court and
other City departments, which, owing to the
City's rapid growth and consequent need of
greater accommodation for constantly expand-
ing public business, had been forced to find
lodgment elsewhere.

Pending the carrying out of the plans for
the permanent improvement and enlargement
of the City Hall, some $35,000 has been
appropriated by the city and County authorities for the building of four commodious,
rapid transit elevators, to replace the two old
and inadequate cars now running, and arrangements are being made by the Trustees

for the building of two large dynamos to light the handsome building by electricity.

The present City Hall is a model public edifice, and this is universally admitted by all who visit Buffalo; it is a model not only in point of its unusual solidity and beauty and small original cost, but in the perfection of its maintenance. It is governed by a Board of Control, comprising six Commissioners and a superintendent; to the Board, as the supervisory, and the superintendent, as the executive, is due the fact that the City and County Hall in Buffalo lays just claim to being the best kept public building in the country.

GRADE CROSSINGS ABOLISHED.

The year 1896 was prolific in events, to the advantage of Buffalo and in the consummation of many plans for its aggrandizement. Not the least of these great tasks has been the work actually accomplished in the matter of abolishing all crossings at grade, which constituted, for years, the railroad Moloch, upon whose altars were sacrificed many valuable human lives. In the year 1888 the Grade Crossing Commission was created, by act of the Legislature, and Governor David B. Hill named the following to act as commissioners and to serve their fellow-citizens, without compensation: Robert B. Adam, William J. Morgan, George Sandrock, Charles A. Sweet, Edward H. Butler, John B. Weber, Frederick Kendall, Solomon Scheu, James E. Nunan. These gentlemen have served from the time of their appointment until the present day, with the exception of Solomon Scheu and James E. Nunan, deceased.

In 1892, Section 1, of Chapter 345, of the laws of 1888, was amended by adding to the original Grade Crossing Commissions Augustus F. Scheu, James Ryan and Henry D. Kirkover, and this was approved by Governor Roswell P. Flower, April 20, 1892. Their work has been a long, tedious and unselfish one, involving many struggles with powerful corporations and much tedious labor of detail; but the reward of the long years of toil is at hand, and during 1896 there were signed contracts with all the important railroad corporations entering Buffalo, thus securing safety to its citizens and insuring humanity, in the future, from slaughter at grade.

PRACTICAL RESULTS ACCOMPLISHED.

The Michigan-street viaduct, a noble work spanning the entire trackage of the New York Central and other railroads, at Michigan street—an artery of trade which connects the northern part of the city with the equally populous south side—was finished, as was also the lowering of the Central and other tracks below the level of Washington street, and the crossing of the Terrace, by subway. Other labors incident to the accomplishment of the work are being rapidly prosecuted. This viaduct alone cost $113,327,41, and the total cost of the whole tremendous undertaking will approximate $5,000,000. The compiler of this work is indebted to Col. George E. Mann, the capable engineer of the commission, for many of the details here presented. And speaking of railroads, it may be noted, incidentally, as significant of the confidence of railroad people in Buffalo's business prosperity, that following the example of the New York Central, the Lehigh Valley Railroad in 1896, put on a fast train between Buffalo and New York, known as the "Black Diamond," which very nearly parallels, in point of time, the achievements of the "Empire State Express," the fastest regular passenger train operating on any railroad in the world.   The Erie Railroad, also, has made an attempt to bid for the through passenger traffic, by shortening their time between this city and New York, and offering a better service.

THE NEW FREE LIBRARY.

Early in the present year a magnificent collection of books, pamphlets, etc., of the Young Men's Association, known as the Buffalo Library, was made free to every respectable citizen of Buffalo, enabling each to draw two books and to keep them out for a limited length of time, subject to the rules and regulations of the association.   An act was drawn, submitted to the Common Council, passed by both branches and approved by the Mayor, which has received the sanction of the Legislature, the signature of the Governor, and become a law.   Henceforth, Buffalo will have one of the finest free-library systems in the country, for the Buffalo Library is noted, far and wide, for the excellence of its collections and the substantial comfort of its reading and study rooms.

THE CHILDREN'S ROOM.

One of the most attractive spots in the building is that known as the children's room, and its usefulness will be in the future much enhanced. The walls are bright with pictures and colored prints. At one end of the room is a bookcase filled with the literature dear to children's hearts, who read with delight the story of "Jack and the Bean Stalk," "Hop O' My Thumb," and "Beauty and the Beast," while the one Brownie book is simply read into tatters, the price it has to pay for its popularity. The room was opened last July, and has proved a greater success than even its projectors hoped. It is of the children, for the children, and by the children. That they appreciate their privileges is demonstrated by the fact that the average daily attendance, between the hours of 2.45 and 6 p. m., is 140. On Saturdays, when the hours are from 9 a. m. to 6 p. m., the largest number recorded for any one day is 762. The room is in charge of Miss Hannah Fernald, who studied library work at Pratt Institute in preparation for her present position. She is devoted to the work, and in her daily contact with the children gains an influence for good over them.

THE HOME OF THE BOOKS.

The Library is housed in a home of its own built some years ago, opposite the Soldiers'

Monument, and facing upon Washington street and Broadway. The architecture of this beautiful pile is unique, and built, as it was, for the purposes for which it is occupied, the building in every way fulfills public requirements. Heretofore, it was a public library only in the sense that admission to its rooms was free, as was the use, on its premises, of books and periodicals. The Municipal Committee taking the initial steps in this matter, and under whose auspices it was carried through, was composed of the following members of the city government: Aldermen Maischoss, Boeckel, Smither, Summers and Kissinger, and Councilmen Klinck, Zipp, Ash, Utley and Keller, His Honor, Edgar B. Jewett, Mayor, and Mark S. Hubbell, City Clerk. This valuable library contains 84,000 volumes, of which five thousand are in the German language.

OTHER BUFFALO LIBRARIES.

Besides the Buffalo Library, there is the Grosvenor, also occupying a home of its own, on the corner of Edward and Franklin streets, but this is contradistinct from the Buffalo Library because its collections are rather special than general in their character, and constitute more an admirable reference library. Notable among collections maintained by private associations are those of the Catholic Institute, on Main street; the German Young Men's Association, housed in Music Hall; Buffalo Historical Society, Buffalo Medical Library Association, Erie County Medical Society, Erie Railway Library Association, Guard of Honor, Harugari Library, Lutheran Young Men's Association, North Buffalo Catholic Association, St. Michael's Young Men's Sodality, Women's Educational and Industrial Union, Young Men's Catholic Association, and the Young Men's Christian Association.

The National Educational Association, which convened in Buffalo last July, surpassed in success any convention held before by that body. The admirable manner in which the 15,000 guests were housed and entertained was an undoubted factor in deciding the G. A. R. to hold its meeting here.

THE TEACHERS' RETIREMENT FUND.

Buffalo has taken her place among the most progressive cities in securing the passage of an act creating a teachers' retirement fund for those who are worn out in the service. The Women Teachers' Association took active part in urging the passage of this bill, and the fact that 900 teachers voted for it undoubtedly helped to push it through. Teachers give one per cent. of their salaries in support of this fund. The expenses of the N. E. A. convention were less than estimated, and after everything was paid it was voted to contribute this unused balance of $2,700 as a nucleus for this pension fund for teachers.

WOMEN IN PUBLIC INSTRUCTION.

The Women's Educational and Industrial Union owns its own building, with a handsome public hall attached, on Niagara Square. It has existed for 12 years, and with each year enlarges its field of usefulness. It is a union of all classes and conditions of women, in which there is none so rich that she has no needs, and none so poor that she cannot serve another. The work of the Union is thoroughly practical, and last year it found employment for 776 women. Its domestic training department is proving what scientific methods can do to exalt household service. Classes have been formed for instruction in cooking, laundry work, dining-room work, and general housekeeping. There are many educational classes and entertainments in literary subjects. The Union also does protective

and philanthropic work.   It has 929 annual
members, 25 sustaining members, and 17 life
members, making a total membership of 971.

THE GREATEST GRAIN PORT.

There are 37 grain elevators in the city of
Buffalo.   These have a total storage capacity
of 17,000,000 bushels.   There are in addition
six transfer towers and eight floating elevators, making a total of 53 elevating buildings,
easily valued at $11,000,000.   An idea of the
present enormous transfer capacity may be
gained from the fact that they are able to
handle 5,000,000 bushels every 24 hours.   The
capacity of the enormous flouring mills of
Buffalo is put at 9,000 barrels per day, and
this they can easily exceed.

The receipts of iron ore at this port last year
were 443,073 net tons.

The shipments of coal at this port last year
amounted to 2,400,068 tons.

UNITED STATES POST-OFFICE TESTIMONY.

The sale of postage stamps for December,
1896, were the largest in the history of the
office, amounting to $69,266.54.   The sales of
postage stamps for the corresponding month
in 1895 aggregated $59,530.98, showing an in-
crease of $9,735.56.   The total stamp sales for

the year 1896 were $712,363.13, which, compared with the sales for the year 1895, shows an increase of $40,554.11.

THE SCHOOL OF PEDAGOGY.

The University of Buffalo took an important step in advancing educational interests in this city when it established in 1895 the School of Pedagogy. There is a growing conviction that teaching no less than law and medicine is a science and should be treated as such. The school occupies the lecture rooms of the Buffalo Library. There are 150 students enrolled, a large increase over last year. Among them are a good many school principals and teachers of long experience, others who wish to prepare themselves to teach, and still others who attend the lectures purely for the pleasure and benefit derived. One of the special features is the attention paid to psychology and child study. This department is supplied with apparatus for measuring the intellectual capacity of the child. So delicate is the instrument that it registers time to the 200th part of a second. Dr. Frank M. McMurry is the principal of the School of Pedagogy. The other professors are: M. V. O'Shea, Rev. Herbert Gardiner Lord, Dr.

Woods Hutchinson, Dr. Ida C. Bender, Dr. James Wright Putnam, and Madam Natalie Mankell. The School of Pedagogy has at its disposal a thoroughly-equipped model school, where students have an opportunity to observe excellent teaching, as well as to place themselves under the criticism of skilled instructors.

UNLIMITED WATER SUPPLY.

The Water Department is a branch of the municipal government, entirely self-supporting, and earning every year more than its expenditures on mains, etc., which it is constantly building, and reserving the rest for the extending of water facilities in the future. Thousands upon thousands of dollars are expended by this department yearly in laying mains through the constantly-increasing list of new streets.

In 1893 a reservoir was constructed on the so-called Dodge Farm, at Best and Jefferson streets, costing $406,000, and with a capacity of 125,000,000 gallons.

In 1896 a new 30,000,000 gallon, triple expansion, Hammond engine was constructed for the City by the Lake Erie Engineering Works; and two new supply mains, one 36-

inch, in Utica street, and one 48-inch, in North street, were laid at an expense of $300,- 000.

POLICE AND FIRE.

Buffalo has the best police and fire departments in the United States. There are 704 men in all in the police employ, and 443 constitute the total number of employes in the fire department. Both departments are governed by boards of commissioners of three; of the former, the Mayor being, ex officio, a member.

THE NEW OFFICE BUILDINGS.

Buffalo is already famous for its rapid growth in new and elegant office buildings, many constructed with foreign capital, which goes to show that Buffalo is banked on by shrewd and thinking men in all parts of the country, from New England and New York to Chicago and other moneyed centers of the West.

And there is a lesson to be learned from the stories of its new buildings, which is that wherever progress constructs new buildings fortune sends tenants to occupy them ; the tendency of the majority of mankind is toward betterment of their surroundings, and the croakers who predicted that Buffalo was having an epidemic of office edifices, and that they would find no tenants, have seen every one of them nearly fully rented before the roofs were fairly trussed upon their walls.

THE LESSON OF THE PAST.

And the old buildings! Like the sinking ships of the sailors' tradition, they are more or less tenantless, and sooner or later, impelled thereto by motives of personal expediency, their owners will tear them down and replace them with new and modern structures, which will not fail to find their occupants, until finally the old rookeries shall have disappeared forever. This is an incident in the history of growth.

Niagara power, the most marvelous natural agent ever chained to the treadmill of human industry, has been converted to the uses of mankind, and in another portion of this volume will be found the franchise alluded to above, which was finally accepted by the Niagara Falls Power Company on the 14th day of January, 1896, by formal documents filed with the City Clerk.

Buffalo, owing to its propinquity to the great Pennsylvania coal fields, has always

58   COMMON COUNCIL MANUAL.

been able to procure fuel for its manufacturers at prices much lower than less favored and more distant cities. Niagara power is under contract to be delivered *for general use,* within these city limits inside of six months, and already the street railways of the city use the Falls power exclusively.

THE CHEAPEST POWER ON EARTH.

With a fuel which must be supplied at much less than the cost of coal and the use of which will necessarily dispense with the labor now necessary in handling, at individual furnaces, the product of the mines, the output of Buffalo manufacturers should, in equal ratio with the decrease in the cost of its production, undersell, in the markets of the world, the goods made in any other city.

So the great task of harnessing Niagara is an accomplished fact, and the Falls, unblemished in their beauty, still present their vision of majesty, being at the same time literally converted to the uses of mankind.

This is a short story of the city, past and present, and, as was said of last year's Manual: "It is not a boom publication, neither is it an exaggeration. All facts are stated with ac-

curacy, and aim at supplying in a small
space as much information as can be used on a
great subject. ''

MARK S. HUBBELL.

Buffalo, N. Y., March 18th, 1897.

BUFFALO IN BRIEF.

Hotels, 48.

Theaters, 10.

Public Markets, 5.

Population, 389,138.

Total square miles, 42.

Sinking Fund, $541,816.18.

Largest flour depot in the world.

Total paved streets, 324.115 miles.

Total acreage of City, 25,343$\frac{576}{1000}$.

Total indebtedness, $12,779,210.66.

Largest sheep market in the world.

Largest horse market in the world.

Natural gas for fuel purposes, unlimited.

Manufactories, 3,000. Over 75,000 operatives.

Parks, 942½ acres.   Park driveways, 19 miles.

Buffalo is the fourth commercial city in the world.

Under contract for 1897, 30 streets for asphalt.

Number of Electric Lights, 2,500; number of gas lamps, 5,856.

Buffalo is the largest city between **New York and Chicago.**

Pavements; Relative cost per square yard: Asphalt, $2.50; brick, 2.40.

Street Railway Percentage Revenue (Law now repealed), $45,613.73 per annum.

Buffalo is the **Second Largest City** in the Empire State, Greater New York being first.

Telephone Rates, $30 for 300 messages; $50 for 500 messages, and $75 for 1,000 messages.

Largest coal trestle in the world, owned by the D. L. & W. Railway. One mile in length.

Financial institutions: Staple and plentiful. Available capital unlimited. Policy liberal.

Water Department owned by City. Valuation, $13,000,000. Bonded Indebtedness, $3,500,000. Cheapest water rate in the United States. High-pressure service.

Electrical power from Niagara Falls now being used in Buffalo. (See franchise and contract elsewhere.)

Street Railways, 150 miles. More under course of construction. All operated and heated by electric-trolley system.

The total receipts of Grain and Flaxseed, by lake, in 1896, were, in bushels, 172,476,664, or the largest amount known in the history of the city.

Pavements, in miles. There are now laid of macadam, 1; stone, 117.598; stone resurfaced with asphalt, 1.806; brick, 4,765; asphalt, 197.629.

More **smooth pavements** than Paris, Washington, London or any other city reported. **In process of construction or ordered:** Asphalt, 14.60 miles.

Cost of electric light, $100.00 per lamp per year, or 30 cents per lamp per night for 365 nights, for public lamps on streets. No "moonlight schedule."

Water, unlimited and pure from Lake Erie, at head of Niagara River, outside of contamination line; capacity of pumping station 145,000,000 gallons per day.

Street Railways: Percentage paid the city on gross earnings, under $1,500,000, two per cent. ; under $2,000,000, two and one-half per cent., and over $2,000,000, three per cent.

Buffalo bonds command higher prices in the market, and are more sought, than those of any other city. There has never been default in payment of interest or principal on any Buffalo security.

What Chief Cuthbertson (U. S. Weather Bureau) Says: " During the 16 days of hot weather, beginning August 1st, 1896, I took observations which showed that out of 18 large cities Buffalo was the coolest.

U. S. Post Office Testimony. The sales of postage stamps for December, 1896, were $69,266.54, the largest in the history of the office. The total stamp sales for the year 1896 were $712,363.13, showing an increase over 1895 of $40,554.11.

The Buffalo Hotel Company. There was incorporated at Albany, on December 2d, 1896, with a capital stock of $300,000, a company, to build, in Buffalo, a handsome, new hotel. It is understood plans have been drawn and a site selected.

Buffalo Schools, 60. The new Masten Park high school will soon be completed, thus giving the city two fine buildings for high-school work. Sites for grammar schools have been purchased and new buildings will be erected as speedily as possible.

The Pan-American Exposition will be held on Cayuga Island in 1899, and the exposition will occupy the entire island, funds for erecting the buildings on which will be raised by the sale of $5.00 bonds, entitling the holders to an ownership interest in the enterprise.

Steam Railroad Trackage. The New York Sun is authority for the following: "Greater New York will have within its limits 464 miles of car tracks; Philadelphia has 400 miles; St. Louis, 291; Baltimore, 255; San Francisco, 231; Chicago, 593, and Buffalo about 600."

Steam railways, 26; 250 passenger trains per day. Over 600 miles of trackage in the city limits. In this respect Buffalo heads the procession, before Greater New York, Chicago, Philadelphia, St. Louis, Baltimore and San Francisco, as computed by the "New York Sun."

Lowest Death Rate. Average 1896, 12.72 per 1,000 of population. Week ending January

11th, 1896, 9.60 per 1,000; corresponding week of 1895, 15.68 per 1,000. Death rate for February, 1896, 29 days, 10.61 per 1,000, as opposed to February, 1895, when the rate was 15.58 per 1,000.

Revenue from Licenses, etc. Department of Excise, $517,011.29; licenses issued by the Mayor, including those other than liquor licenses, as peddlers, pawnbrokers, theatrical, etc., $29,823.00. Total license receipts, all sources, for 1896, $546,834.29, or about 22 per cent. of the municipal revenue, or 15 per cent. of tax receipts.

The Entries and Clearances at the port of Buffalo for 1896 were exceedingly large, in fact, they are the largest ever recorded here. The total number of entries during 1896 was 5,581, the tonnage being 5,617,494 tons. Total clearances foot up 5,740, with a tonnage of 5,670,032 tons.

A New Theater. There will be ready for use when the fall theatrical season opens, the beautiful, new place of amusement, being constructed, at large expense, on the corner of Mohawk and Washington streets, by Louis H. Eckhert. The plans show a fire-proof structure, beautifully planned, and in the highest degree modern and convenient.

Valuation of Property. The increase in the total of assessed valuation of the real and personal property for the years 1897-8 is $4,520,945. The total valuation of all property in Buffalo (assessors' estimate) is $265,000,000, including property valued at $25,000,000, exempt from execution. Personal property estimated $15,000,000.

One Death from Sun-stroke. "The one man who died from sun-stroke, in Buffalo, during the deadly heated term of last year, when deaths, daily, from heat prostration were common in all other American cities, was Martin Hecker, brewery collector, who succumbed August 6th. Buffalo is not a sun-stroke city." Dr. Wende, Health Commissioner.

Grand Opera in Buffalo. Straws show which way the wind blows: Abbey, Schoeflin & Grau brought the entire Metropolitan Opera House Company to Buffalo, in 1896, including Melba, Nordica, the DeRetzskes, and others, for a three-nights season, and scored a decided financial success. Buffalo is the only city as yet thus favored between New York and Chicago.

An Expert's Opinion. Dr. Albert H. Gihon, of the United States Navy, says: "Buffalo is

SEVENTY-FOURTH REGIMENT ARMORY.

always in the lead in sanitary matters. The other cities are forced to follow. In many ways Buffalo has little to do, for in some lines she is nearly perfect. The arrangements and methods are invariably the best, and I no longer wondered at the low death rate when I saw how your city takes care of the Buffalo health.''

The Seventy-fourth Regiment Armory. The State of New York is under pledge to expend $400,000 in the erection of an armory for the Seventy-fourth Regiment, upon Niagara street, on the site occupied by the old reservoir, and conditionally donated to the State for this purpose. This building is now actually in course of contruction, and will be one of the handsomest buildings of this kind in the country.

Cool and Comfortable. The Brocton Mirror says: ''Buffalo is classed as one of the large cities of the country, and, while people were dropping down dead from heat in the streets of almost every other large city in the country, the mortality in the Bison City was little if any greater than in country districts while the torrid wave lasted. People living along the lower shores of Lake Erie have much to be thankful for.''

A $10,000,000 Harbor Improvement Company. A bill was introduced into the Legislature, Feb. 25, by Assemblyman Schneider to incorporate "The South Buffalo Harbor Improvement and Ship Canal Co., to define its rights, etc." It is understood this company proposes to build ship canals, acquire river and harbor frontages, and in other ways demonstrate the confidence of its shareholders in the wisdom of Buffalo investments.

Cost of gas, 17 cents per lamp per month, to light, extinguish, clean and keep in repair. Street lamps to be lighted and kept lighted for an aggregate of not less than 3,951½ hours in each year. Pro-rata reduction to be made for such hours as any of said lamps are shown to have been not lighted. Requirements of street gas lamps, four feet of gas per hour. Average required equal to 18 candles per light. Rates of gas to private consumers, $1.00 per 1,000 feet net.

To pave a street in Buffalo it is necessary that a petition be presented to the Common Council, asking that it be paved with the material desired, which petition must be certified by the Assessors as containing the signatures of a majority of the resident property owners, representing at least two-fifths of the frontage; if it is desired to pave as a sanitary measure, petitions not being obtainable, this may be done by order of the Common Council on a two-thirds vote.

The "Senator." A new, all-steel boat, of channel construction, built by the Detroit Dry Dock Company and launched July 25th, 1896, will bring grain to Buffalo. She is one of the largest ships ever launched on fresh waters, being 424 feet long, 45 feet six inches beam and 28 feet wide; her tonnage is 4,048 gross, 3,178 net. She is divided by five watertight, steel bulkheads, thus enabling her to either carry a grain or a general cargo. She has a capacity of 278,000 bushels of oats.

Asphalt by Whom Laid. Since 1882 streets have been paved by the various companies with smooth pavement as follows: By the A. L. Barber Asphalt Paving Company (Trinidad Lake asphalt), 193.79 miles, comprising 247 streets or parts of streets. The German Rock Asphalt & Cement Co. (also laying Barber asphalt), 36.77 miles. The Standard Paving Co., laying Kentucky bituminous rock, 17 miles—a total of 247.56 miles of smooth pavement, which includes some private streets used, but not dedicated to the city.

The Federal Post Office. Foundations have been laid and work is being prosecuted upon the superstructure of one of the handsomest post-office buildings in the United States, now being erected by the Federal Government, and which will occupy the entire block bounded by Ellicott, Oak, Swan and South Division streets. This noble structure will cost $2,000,000, and, although work prosecuted by the National Government is usually slow at arriving at completion, it is fair to believe that by 1903 Buffalo may boast of one of the most handsome government buildings in the country.

A 3,000,000-Bushel All-Steel Elevator. The Northern Steamship Company has secured a site on the City Ship Canal, opposite the foot of Ganson Street, and bids have been let for the construction of the largest grain elevator, but one, in the United States. D. A. Robinson, of Chicago, will have charge of the work of construction. The excavating for the foundations was begun on Feb. 26th, 1897. This structure will be 395 feet long, 120 feet wide and 160 feet high. It will be the first steel structure of the kind in the United States; its construction will call for 7,000 tons of material; its cost will be $400,000, and the building will be steel from bottom up, and even the bins will be lined with that material.

What Dundee Says. A writer in The Dundee (Scotland) Advertiser, of December 1st, 1896, who had evidently been to Buffalo, said : " The ports at the head of the lakes may ship more grain than Buffalo, but Buffalo handles it twice over. Most of the trunk lines from New York find it necessary to run their own fleets of steamers on the lakes. Outside of Washington, there is no city in the United States to compare with Buffalo in residential charms, combined with plain comfort; and the most modern system of transportation combines the lake and rail routes, and Buffalo has become their point of union. In this respect it has unique advantages, raising it above all other lake ports beyond reach of rivalry. "

The London Times, in November last, treating of Niagara power said : "The Thunderer knows a good thing when it sees it. It is safe to predict that it is only a question of time, and no very great time, when all the industries in Buffalo requiring power will receive it from Niagara Falls, and that the 22 miles separating the two cities will be built solid with smokeless and teeming factories, and that this region will become the greatest manufacturing center on the American continent. Thus another imperishable laurel is added to the Victorian era.''

During the past year there were built nearly a score of large steel vessels, involving the investment of over $3,000,000, capable to meet the demands of the carrying trade between Buffalo and the Upper Lakes; they have a capacity of transporting 1,400,000 tons of iron ore, from the Upper Lake ports to the East, via Buffalo, during a season.

Markets self-sustaining. The increment from the markets of the City of Buffalo exceeds the cost of operating the same, and has shown a revenue, during the past two years, of $1,000 per month.

A STUDY IN ENUMERATION.

The statement below will answer many questions propounded through the mails, concerning Buffalo's population, past and present.

Since 1820, the National Government has taken, every ten years, a census which showed as results, regarding Buffalo, the following figures:

1820...... 2,095........39th city in the United States.
1830...... 8,668........23d " " " " "
1840...... 18,213........18th " " " " "
1850...... 42,261........13th " " " " "
1860...... 81,129........10th " " " " "
1870......117,714........11th " " " " "
1880......155,134 ....14th " " " " "
1890......255,664........11th " " " " "

These are the National censuses taken since Buffalo became a city, in every decade, and there has been a vast accretion to the growth of the city, since the last National enumeration.

A State census, taken in 1892, made Buffalo's population, in round numbers, 284,000.

A Police census, taken by the City in May, 1895, gave the figures as 335,709, and this was in the latter part of May, when vast numbers of persons claiming Buffalo as their residence, and actually residing here eight months out of the twelve, had left the city upon business which keeps them absent during the summer months.   A May census is no just criterion of the population of such a city as Buffalo, the maritime interests of which keep thousands of its population absent from the city during much of the season of navigation.

It is here shown the population of Buffalo far exceeds the 375,000 inhabitants, by some last year believed to be an over-sanguine estimate.

The City Directory, published in 1896, contained 109,750 names, which for that year, calculating with a multiple of three and one-half, the usual factor in such cases, gives a quotient for 1896, of 384,125.

Now, New York city, with an enormous floating population, and a concededly large population of unattached persons—those without families—according to the Times of that city, uses the number five as the multiple, which, of course, in the case of Buffalo, would swell our population nearly 200,000 more; but three and one-half is the accepted multiple.

THE MOST CENTRAL SHIPPING POINT IN THE COUNTRY.

Another way at arriving at the population is by finding the accurate multiple to be used in connection with the total number of persons registered at the last Presidential election, which, in Buffalo, was 65,692. Using the multiple six gives a quotient of 394,152, which—taking into account the fact that Buffalo's foreign-born and still unnaturalized population is probably larger than that of any other city in the Union, proportionate to its size, as shown by the fact that thousands of aliens, every year, swing into line and become voters—is a most conservative multiple to use, since seven and six are quite commonly employed in this connection.

The concensus of all which calculations make it entirely reasonable to state that the conservative estimate of Buffalo's population—the population of a city essentially of homes—lies somewhere between the result of the directory estimate and the result of the registration estimate, a mean between which extremes makes the grand total 389,138.

Other factors are collateral and corroborative of these calculations. The testimony of the post office, the story of the directory, the calculation on the registration lists, all point to the conclusion that Buffalo's population has always been under, rather than overstated, for it is learned from the United States Postal authorities that, while Buffalo has 170 regular letter carriers—and more have been asked for—its next nearest competitors, Detroit and Cleveland, have a lesser number, the wants of the former city being supplied by 146 carriers, and of the latter by 161 carriers. These calculations are based upon plain and convincing figures, without any attempt to be anything but fair in the matter, and to arrive at as near an approximation to the truth as possible, which places this subject upon a plane beyond cavil and where everybody can make their own calculations and reach the same results.

And it should be remembered in considering the directory estimates that the multiple three and one-half is used upon the directory of 1896, and it is fair to assume that that of 1897 will add some thousands of names to the total of 1896.

THE GIANT "NIAGARA."

The Mighty Cataract Subjugated to the Uses of Mankind—The Birth of the Power Spirit.

In 1886, public-spirited citizens of Buffalo offered a reward of $100,000 in cash to that master genius who should devise practicable plans for "harnessing" Niagara. That reward found no claimant, and for years the subject lay quiescent, but the seed sown by that offer fell on fertile ground, and set to work that veritable mammoth of the ages, the scientific human brain, and as a result, in the year 1890, a company was formed, known as the Niagara Falls Power Company, headed by such masters of finance as D. O. Mills, Francis Lynde Stetson, Edward D. Adams, Edward A. Wickes, William B. Rankine and John Jacob Astor.

The idea of the men who offered the $100,-000 contemplated the use of the power of the Niagara torrent at or close to the gates of Buffalo ; but this company went further afield and conceived the tremendous project of chaining to commerce the Niagara Cataract.

FORGING THE FETTERS

There loomed before the promulgators of this bold enterprise the difficulty, not only of the actual utilizing of the cataract, but, further, and more commanding in its apparent impossibility, the problem of transmitting, once harnessed, that marvelous energy, without so great an expense as to make the use of it impracticable to manufacturers, and without so great a loss of energy in its transmission as to render the power delivered at the other end of the line of insignificant proportions; but all these obstacles were overcome—how, is a matter of history—and on the 16th day of November, 1896, a little group of interested persons and citizens, who had been invited to be present, were gathered at midnight in the great Power House of the Buffalo Railway Company, on Niagara street, waiting for the little finger of the giant power of Niagara to be placed on a piece of ingenious electrical mechanism in the City of Buffalo and to bid it revolve—the impulse came—and thus Buffalo and Niagara Falls were wedded. Those who were in the power house when the current was turned on and the first volt received were: George Urban, Jr., president of the Cataract Power & Conduit Company; Charles R. Huntley, general manager of the same company ; Mayor Jewett ; Spencer S. Kingsley, president of the Buffalo Real Estate Exchange ; Henry M. Watson, president of the Buffalo Railway Company, and half a dozen others.

HOW THE POWER WAS FIRST RECEIVED.

The story of the accomplished achievement was told in these graphic terms in the columns of a newspaper the next day :

"Then the coil in one of the big black machines began to turn. It started with steady, easy revolutions. A splutter of sparks, blue and white and yellow, flashed from it. There was a scratching sound, like sandpaper scraping hard wood. Then came a heavy buzz. Faster and faster whirled the coil. The buzz thickened into a rushing roar. The vision blurred in following the circling coil and the big machine seemed to be motion-less, so fast did the converter work. Not a tremble, not a quiver, only a great roaring black mass, with the center rushing round and round in a wild whirl. The watchers gazed in silence for a moment. Then they began to applaud. Then they laughed de-lightedly and shook hands. Outside a cannon boomed. Its explosion sounded like a mere tapping of the heel on a carpeted floor to those inside the power house. Louder buzzed the big converter. The alternating ammeter showed 200 volts at the end of 45 seconds. In two minutes, the indicator had passed 350 volts and was trembling on toward 400. In just four minutes and 30 seconds, it touched 550 volts. The watchers moved back to talk it over. The Niagara power was in Buffalo at last.''

THE HARVEST OF PERSISTENT ENDEAVOR.

At the moment when the first premonitory thrill was felt in the transmitter at Buffalo, and the first appulse given to the dynamo in the street railway company's power house, the union of Buffalo and Niagara Falls was completed, and a miracle of science was accomplished. To send a few words, by an electric current, under three thousand miles of ocean was a great deed in its day, but to transmit the tremendous forces of Niagara over 27 miles of upland and lowland, to turn the wheels of industry in Buffalo, was more marvelous still.

For years, the mightiest geniuses of the electrical world had centered their attention upon the Niagara problem, and scientists of

all nations had sought as eagerly for the
answer to the riddle as did ever the alchemists
of old to transmute the baser metals into gold,
and most of them had sought in vain—but
not all.

THE WIZARD, TESLA.

A gaunt, young seer, with dark and brood-
ing eyes, first saw through the mist and
doubts of the future, the truth shining forth
serene and clear: This was Nikola Tesla.
He had predicted, years before, that the
transmission of power from the Niagara
Cataract to Buffalo was as certain as the
rising of the sun next morning, and his
confidence in the future of this section of
country was absolute from the moment when
the possibility of practical electrical transmission became clear in his mind. He
became identified with the men interested in
the power project and worked for many
months on his idea. Later when his dream
was nearly realized, in a newspaper inter-
view, July 20, 1896, he said: ''This power
plant is one of the wonders of this century,
it is a marvel in its completeness and in its
superiority of construction. When it shall
be in full operation the results in many
ways will be wonderful, will be surpris-

ing to those who have doubted that such things could be accomplished. In its entirety, in connection with Buffalo and the possibilities of the future, the plant and the prospect of future development in electrical science, are my ideals. They are what I have long anticipated and have labored in an insignificant way to contribute toward bringing about, and this wonderful development of electric power will make Buffalo the greatest city in the world, if I mistake not. The possibilities are unknown and unlimited. Buffalo must in time reap advantages from this wonderful development of power, which none of us dare guess, and which even the most far-seeing cannot anticipate. The first effects naturally will be to the advantage of the Falls. But Buffalo will be the greatest reaper of benefits. The result of this great development of electric power will be that the two cities will reach out their arms and will join each other and become one grand municipality. United they will form the greatest city in the world.''

AN ELECTRIC BANQUET.

**The Unique Dinner at the Ellicott Club in Buffalo
which Celebrated the Advent of
Niagara Power.**

On January 12, 1897, summoned by invitation of the Cataract Power & Conduit Company, there gathered in the banquet hall of the Ellicott Club, in Buffalo—a banquet hall unequaled in beauty and spaciousness in the country, and occupying a commanding position on the top floor of the largest office building in the world—from all points in the United States, men learned in science and distinguished in letters, already signalized by their brilliant deeds and daring enterprise, to banquet with the Power Company, in celebration of the great event before described. Covers were laid for 350 guests, and there were no vacant chairs.

The banquet was the blossom of prophecy, and the banqueters hailed, by their presence, the inauguration of a new era for Buffalo, The Age of Electricity.

DISTINGUISHED GUESTS.

At this banquet, George Urban, Jr., Charles R. Huntley and William B. Rankine, all of the Niagara Falls Power Company, did the honors; and there were seated at the guest table with them Francis Lynde Stetson, of New York, representing the interest in the power enterprise of millions of metropolitian capital; Nikola Tesla, the electrical wizard of the world; Charles F. Brush, father of the Brush Electric Light system; Frank Sprague, inventor of the electric trolley; Elihu Thompson, of Lynn, Mass.; William Stanley, of Pittsburg, one of the first believers in the alternating current, and an inventor of no mean ability; T. Cummerford Martin, editor of the *Electric Engineer* of New York city, and many others of equal distinction.

LOCAL ELECTRIC PIONEERS.

It may be said, while on the subject of electricity, although not entirely germain to the power subject, that James Adams may, practically, be called the father of practical electricity in Buffalo, and with Daniel O'Day and John M. Brinker, was the first investor of substantial capital in the business of electric lighting in this city. Of these three, Mr.

O'Day's name stands forth pre-eminent as the generous and farsighted investor of large amounts in electric-light and Standard-Oil enterprises, and one of the master stockholders in the Niagara Falls Power Company.

It is regretable that space forbids more extended excerpts from speeches made on that memorable occasion ; suffice it to say, however, that the concensus of opinion there expressed was to the effect that Buffalo stands upon the threshold of conquest and is destined to unequaled precedence in the procession of cities. At that banquet of giants the arch-wizard, Tesla, said, among other things :

HIS DREAM CAME TRUE.

"In the great enterprise at Niagara we see not only a bold engineering and commercial feat, but far more, a giant stride in the right direction, as indicated both by exact science and philanthropy. Its success is a signal for the utilization of water powers all over the world, and its influence upon industrial development is incalculable. This fortunate city herself is to be congratulated. With resources so unequaled, with commercial facilities and advantages such as few cities in the world possess, and with the enthusiasm and progressive spirit of its citizens, it is sure to become one of the greatest industrial centers of the globe."

And it should be remembered that this man, Tesla, was the one electrical genius of the world who insisted, against the stress of the opinions of others, then more famous, that electrical power generated at Niagara Falls could, through the alternating current, be transmitted for manufacturing purposes to Buffalo, with so small a loss of energy as to make it salable in this city at a lower price than power generated by steam, and earn a substantial increment to its projectors.

AMOUNTS PAID FOR LICENSES.

The Low Rates Imposed on Those Doing Business Under Buffalo City Ordinances.

Auctioneers, $50 per year.
Butchers, $15 per year.
Billposters, $50 per year.
Fish Dealers, $10 per year.
Junk Dealers—
   Wholesale, $25 per year.
   With horse, $3 per year.
   On foot , $1 per year.
Pawnbrokers, $250 per year.
Billiard or pool tables and bowling alleys, $5
   per year, each.
Peddlers, $2 to $4 per month.
Plumbers, $10 per year.
Shows, theatres, $50 per year.
Music Playing on street, $2 per month.
Vault cleaners, $50 per year.
Collectors of Dead Animals, $50 per year.
Wagons—
   Team, $5 per year.
   One horse, $1 per year.
   Hack and Carriage, $5 per year.

SUGGESTIVE FIGURES ABOUT BUFFALO.

From the date of its incorporation until 1870 the Buffalo censuses, taken together, on an average, showed a growth of 20,000 every 10 years, or 2,000 a year.

From 1880 to 1890 the population increased from 154,546 to 254,457, or 10,000 a year, and then the race-horse period of growth began.

The following table estimates the phenomenal accretions of later years in rather under than over the correct figures of increase.

1890 to 1891, increase....	20,000
Total..............	274,457
1891 to 1892, increase....	20,000
Total..............	294,457
1892 to 1893, increase...	20,000
Total..............	314,457
1893 to 1894, increase...	20,000
Total..............	334,457
1894 to 1895, increase...	20,000
Total..............	354,457
1895 to 1896, increase...	20,000
Total..............	374,457
1896 to 1897, increase same ratio.............	394,457

Taking the calculation based on a multiplication of the number of persons registered at the last election by the multiple six, the result is 393,522, which came pretty close to demonstrating the accuracy of the above table.

These are round-number figures, and undoubtedly understate the facts. Growth is cumulative. So that it may be stated as a conservative estimate that at the present rate of increase this city will have a population of over half a million inhabitants by 1900, and probably before.

CENSUS PROOFS IN BLACK AND WHITE.

By Decades:

Average 10 years' growth, 1832 to 1880=
20,000 per decade.

1880 to 1890, 10 years' growth, 10,000 a
year=100,000.

By Years:

Average years' growth, between 1832 and
1880—2,000.

One year's growth, 1896 to 1897=20,000.

The rate of growth in any single year since
1890 is hence seen to equal that achieved in
any of the decades prior to 1880, and 1896 is
estimated to have added at least 30,000 to the
population, although the figures in the table
of growth modestly put it at the old rate of
20,000—making the total result as stated,
394,457.

FROM THE WATCH TOWERS OF SCIENCE.

Facts, Figures and Statements Proving Buffalo One of the Healthiest Cities in the World.

Buffalo has a perfectly-equipped Health Department, which is fast becoming a model by which other cities delight to pattern, and with good reason, for its work has borne fruit in a most startling and gratifying manner.

Just where the limits of possibilities end, in respect to the results accomplished by the Department of Health of Buffalo, is difficult to conjecture. It was believed in 1895 that the death rate had reached its minimum, when it stood lower than that of any other city of its size in the world; but the year 1896 established a still more favorable standard. It is the aim of the Department to retain Buffalo permanently in the front rank in this respect, and if vigilance and progressiveness count, then this object will be accomplished.

A brief study of the figures, as taken from the summaries of the Bureau of Vital Statistics, will furnish an interesting object lesson :

THE CHEAPEST POWER IN THE WORLD IS AT BUFFALO.

Year.	No. of Deaths.	Rate per 1,000 Population.
1891	6,001	23.48
1892	5,697	19.98
1893	5,711	19.03
1894	5,260	16.76
1895	4,684	13.95
1896	4,452	12.72

Although the population of Buffalo increased over 100,000 since 1891, yet there has been steady decrease both in the number of deaths and the rate. The former is shown in the following table:

Decrease in deaths over				1891	1,549
"	"	"	"	1892	1,245
"	"	"	"	1893	1,259
"	"	"	"	1894	828
"	"	"	"	1895	232

It has long been observed that the greatest proportionate mortality occurred in children under five years of age, and great efforts have therefore been directed towards lessening the mortality during that period of life. After passing the age of childhood, a Buffalonian's chances for longevity are good. In the past year a great reduction took place in the death rate of infants. Much of this can be attributed to measures adopted by this department.

Circulars giving valuable information on the care of infants are sent to the mothers on the threshold of each summer, instructing them as to means of prevention of summer deseases of infants, and vigorous inspections, reaching to its source, are constantly made of the milk supply, and both producers and dealers are kept under strict supervision.

Consumption in adults and diphtheria in children have long been important factors in the causation of deaths in this and other northern cities; hence it was but natural that extraordinary efforts should be made in this direction.

About two years ago an order was issued by this department requiring physicians to report all cases of pulmonary tuberculosis which came under their care. Circulars pertaining to the mode of infection, comparative isolation and care of patients are sent to those mostly interested, and other means adopted to lessen, as much as possible, the progress of this disease.

Although this may, to a certain extent, be a system of education, yet it in no way conflicts with the prerogatives of the attending physician.

It is gratifying to learn that the City of New York has just adopted similar measures.

Although in such a large city we are never entirely without diphtheria, yet the prevailing system enforced by the department has kept its progress so well in check that it has never been necessary to close up a school on this account. The early diagnosis afforded by the bacteriological examinations has given physicians great advantage in successfully combating this malady, and the results are apparent.

During the year 1896 there were 8,414 births and 2,525 marriages.

Other channels and methods through which this desirable result is sought for may be referred to in emphasizing their import, viz. : the strict enforcement of judicious sanitary ordinances, particularly relating to plumbing and drainage, general sanitary supervision of milk and food supplies, thorough inspection of cattle and markets, etc.

JACOB KISSINGER,
President of the Board of Aldermen

LEGISLATIVE . .

. . BRANCHES

OF THE

CITY GOVERNMENT

FOR 1897.

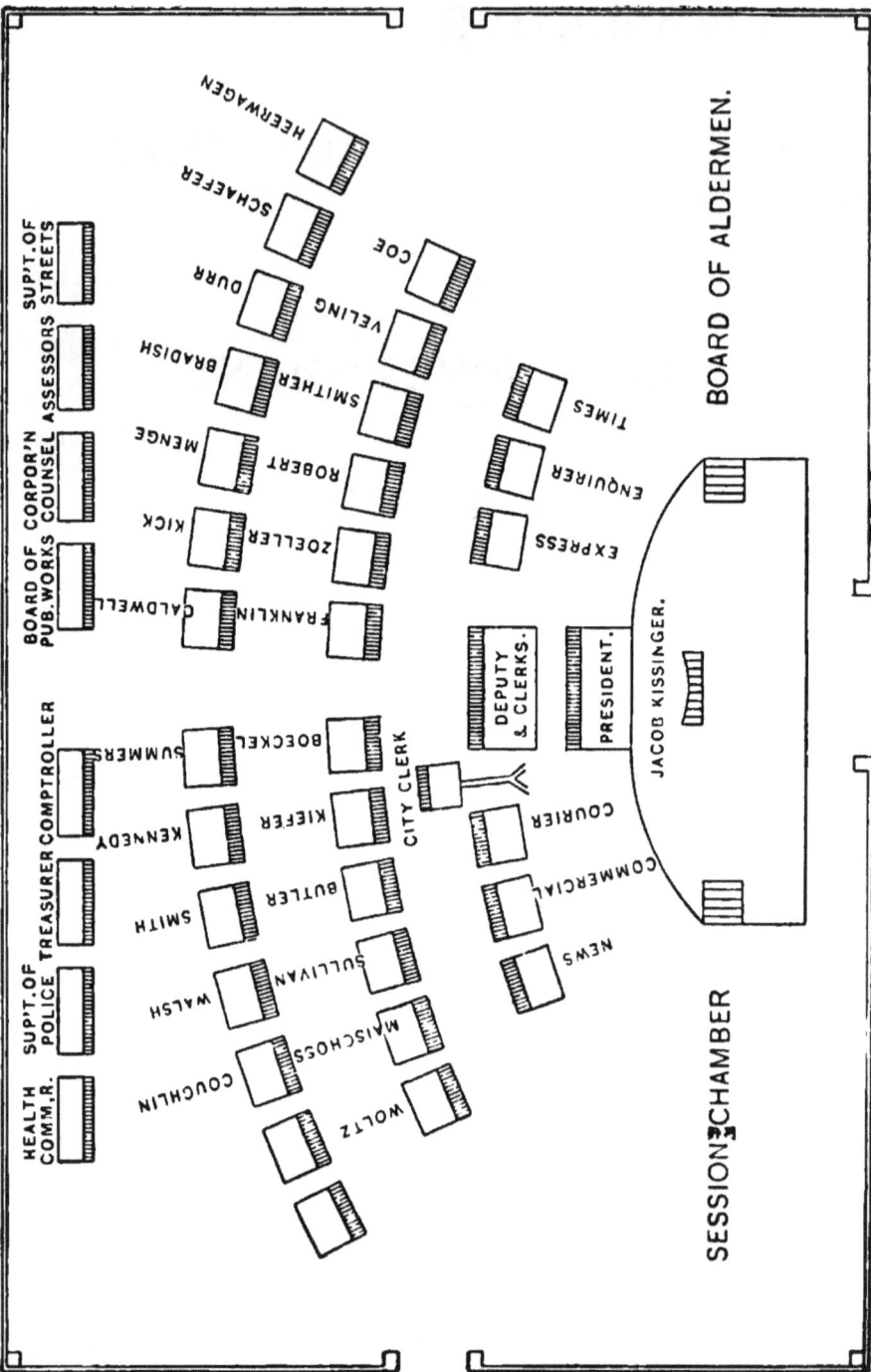

BOARD OF ALDERMEN.

HEALTH COMM.R.   SUPT.OF POLICE   TREASURER   COMPTROLLER   BOARD OF PUB.WORKS   CORPOR'N COUNSEL   ASSESSORS   SUPT.OF STREETS

HEERWAGEN
SCHAEFER
COE
VELING
DURR
SMITHER
BRADISH
MENGE
ROBERT
KICK
ZOELLER
CALDWELL
FRANKLIN
TIMES
ENQUIRER
EXPRESS

SUMMERS
BOECKEL
KENNEDY
KIEFER
SMITH
BUTLER
WALSH
SULLIVAN
MAISCHOSS
COUGHLIN
WOLTZ

CITY CLERK

DEPUTY & CLERKS.

PRESIDENT.

JACOB KISSINGER.

COURIER
COMMERCIAL
NEWS

SESSION CHAMBER

MEMBERS OF THE BOARD OF ALDER-MEN.

Jacob Kissinger, President.

FIRST WARD.

JOHN J. COUGHLIN.—Elected November 5. 1895. Plurality 4. Business, No. 335 Ganson Street. Residence, No. 335 Ganson Street. Telephone, none.

SECOND WARD.

JOHN P. SULLIVAN.—Elected November 6, 1894. Plurality 547. Business, No. 119 Chicago Street. Residence, No. 12 Hamburg Street. Telephone, ''Seneca 1032.''

THIRD WARD.

JOSEPH BUTLER.—Elected November 6, 1894. Plurality 85. Business, No. 204 Seneca Street. Residence same. Telephone, none.

FOURTH WARD.

JOHN WALSH.—Elected November 6, 1894. Plurality 358. Residence No. 213 Van Rensselaer Street. Business 95 Franklin Street. Telephone, ''Seneca 916.

FIFTH WARD.

WILLIAM SUMMERS.—Elected November 6, 1894. Plurality 213. Business, No. 20 Washington Market. Residence, No. 1267 Seneca Street. Telephone, "Hamburg 44-I."

SIXTH WARD.

CHARLES KIEFER.—Elected November 6, 1894. Plurality 168. Business, No. 268 Ellicott Street. Residence, 474 Oak Street. Telephone, "Seneca 1235."

SEVENTH WARD.

EDWARD J. G. SCHAEFER.—Elected November 5, 1895. Plurality 130. Business, No. 168 Ellicott Street. Residence, No. 64 Walnut Street. Telephone, "Seneca 1086."

EIGHTH WARD.

ADAM DURR.—Elected November 5, 1895. Plurality 338. Business, No. 276 Jefferson Street. Residence same. Telephone, none.

NINTH WARD.

JOHN O. G. ROBERT.—Elected November 5, 1895. Plurality 382. Business, No. 191 Sherman Street. Residence, same. Telephone, "Howard 53."

TENTH WARD.

ADAM BOECKEL.—Elected November 6,

1894. Plurality 373. Business, No. 685
Clinton Street. Residence, same. Telephone, "Howard 216."

ELEVENTH WARD.

JAMES SMITH.—Elected November 5, 1895.
Plurality 220. Business, Stock Yards.
Residence, No. 30 Cassy Street. Telephone, "Howard 280."

TWELFTH WARD.

SAMUEL CALDWELL.—Elected November
5, 1895. Plurality 527. Business, No. 338
Pine Street. Residence, same. Telephone, none.

THIRTEENTH WARD.

JOHN KICK.—Elected November 6, 1894.
Plurality 544. Business, No. 475 Adams
Street. Residence, same. Telephone,
none.

FOURTEENTH WARD.

CHARLES P. WOLTZ.—Elected November
5, 1895. Plurality 388. Business, No.
1125 Genesee Street. Residence, same.
Telephone, "Howard 383 A."

FIFTEENTH WARD.

JACOB KISSINGER.—Elected November 5,
1895. Plurality 224. Business, No. 12

Washington Market. Residence, No. 581 Oak Street Telephone, "Seneca 1142."

SIXTEENTH WARD.

FREDERICK A. MENGE.—Elected November 6, 1894. Plurality 440. Business, No. 480 Genesee Street. Residence, same. Telephone, "Howard 200."

SEVENTEENTH WARD.

FREDERICK W. M. HEERWAGEN.—Elected November 5, 1895. Plurality 1,031. Residence, No. 286 Glenwood Avenue. Telephone, none.

EIGHTEENTH WARD.

GEORGE ZOELLER.—Elected November 5, 1895. Plurality 172. Residence, No. 767 Glenwood Avenue. Telephone, none.

NINETEENTH WARD.

JOHN J. KENNEDY.—Elected November 6, 1894. Plurality 335. Business, corner West Eagle and Pearl Streets. Residence, No. 320 Front Avenue. Telephone, "Seneca 581."

TWENTIETH WARD.

JAMES FRANKLIN.—Elected November 6, 1894. Plurality 842. Business, No. 329 Niagara Street. Residence, No. 222 Prospect Avenue. Telephone, "Tupper 56."

TWENTY-FIRST WARD.

FRANK MAISCHOSS.—Elected November 5, 1895. Plurality 995. Business, No. 57 Chicago Street. Residence, No. 64 Day's Park. Telephone, "Seneca 1455."

TWENTY-SECOND WARD.

CLIFFORD S. A. COE.—Elected November 5, 1895. Plurality 802. Business, No. 95 Franklin Street room No. 1. Residence, No. 766 Prospect Avenue. Telephone "Seneca 916."

TWENTY-THIRD WARD.

JOSEPH C. VELING.—Elected November 6, 1894. Plurality 1,134. Residence, No. 169 Eighteenth Street. Telephone, Engine House No. 17, "Seneca 640."

TWENTY-FOURTH WARD.

ROBERT K. SMITHER.—Elected November 5, 1895. Plurality 1,792. Business, No. 588 Niagara Street and No. 279 Bryant Street. Residence, No. 456 Elmwood Avenue. Telephone, "Tupper 241-A and 241-D."

TWENTY-FIFTH WARD.

WILLIAM H. BRADISH.—Elected November 6, 1894. Plurality 620. Business, No. 209 Real Estate Exchange. Telephone "Seneca 153." Residence, No. 162 Dearborn Street. Telephone, "Amherst 12."

STANDING COMMITTEES
OF THE
BOARD OF ALDERMEN.
FOR 1897.

FINANCE—**Smither**, Franklin, Bradish, Summers, Walsh.

ORDINANCES—**Kissinger,** Smither, Boeckel, Bradish, Coe, Summers, Kiefer.

SCHOOLS—**Boeckel,** Maischoss, Robert, Coe, Schaefer, Menge, Kiefer.

STREETS—**Franklin,** Coe, Boeckel, Maischoss, Kick, Caldwell, Summers.

SEWERS—**Woltz,** Schaefer, Heerwagen, Veling, Zoeller, Smith, Walsh.

FIRE—**Menge,** Bradish, Coughlin, Walsh, Butler.

BRIDGES—**Coughlin,** Caldwell, Woltz, Kennedy, Kiefer.

WATER—**Kick,** Schaefer, Franklin, Heerwagen, Smith.

PUBLIC BUILDINGS—**Schaefer,** Veling, Menge, Walsh, Butler.

CLAIMS—**Maischoss,** Smither, Woltz, Bradish, Summers.

POOR—**Zoeller**, Robert, Durr, Woltz, Kiefer.

SIDE AND CROSSWALKS—**Veling**, Coughlin, Zoeller, Sullivan, Smith.

LAMPS—**Heerwagen**, Caldwell, Kick, Coughlin, Kennedy.

TAXES AND ASSESSMENTS—**Bradish**, Durr, Woltz, Butler, Sullivan.

POLICE—**Caldwell**, Franklin, Zoeller, Robert, Kennedy.

SANITARY MEASURES—**Menge**, Franklin, Maischoss, Kiefer, Kennedy.

WHARVES AND HARBORS — **Coe**, Boeckel, Coughlin, Kennedy, Sullivan.

PUBLIC GROUNDS—**Robert**, Heerwagen, Veling, Durr, Smith.

MARKETS—**Maischoss**, Schaefer, Boeckel, Heerwagen, Sullivan.

LICENSES—**Durr**, Veling, Zoeller, Butler, Walsh.

INVESTIGATING—**Smither**, Robert, Caldwell, Summers, Smith.

FOURTH OF JULY—**Bradish**, Kick, Menge, Coe, Butler.

RULES—**Durr**, Smither, Kick, Sullivan and the President.

COMMITTEE MEETINGS.

Regular meetings of the Committees of the Board of Aldermen are scheduled for Thursday nights at 7.30, subject to change by the chairmen. Meetings are announced before adjournment in the Board of Aldermen each Monday.

The announcements are to be found in the official paper each Tuesday at the end of the minutes of the Council proceedings.

ORDER OF BUSINESS

OF THE

BOARD OF ALDERMEN.

1. Reading, correcting and approving the journal of the last session.
2. Communications from the Mayor.
3. Reports and communications from Corporation officers.

   Comptroller.

   Treasurer.

   Corporation Counsel.

   Department of Public Works.

   Department of Health.

   Superintendent of Education.

   Overseer of the Poor.

   Assessors.

   City Clerk.

   Fire Commissioners.

   Department of Police.

108   COMMON COUNCIL MANUAL.

Police Justice.

Miscellaneous Communications.

4. Petitions, Remonstrances and Accounts.

5. Motions, Resolutions and Notices.

6. Reports of Standing Committes.

7. Reports of Special Committees.

8. Committee of the Whole.

9. Unfinished Business.

10. Announcement of Committee Meetings.

11. Adjournment.

CHRISTIAN KLINCK,
President of the Board of Councilmen.

MEMBERS OF THE BOARD OF COUNCIL-MEN.

CHRISTIAN KLINCK, *President.* — Term expires, January 1, 1898. Vote received, 28,913. Business, No. 101 East Market Street. Telephone, "Seneca 391," Packing House Telephone, "Seneca 391 A." Residence, No. 144 Swan Street. Telephone, "Seneca 306."

JAMES N. ADAM. — Term expires January 1, 1900. Vote received, 24,753. Business, No. 389 Main Street. Residence, No. 60 Oakland Place. Telephone, "Seneca 649" and "Bryant 360."

JAMES ASH. — Term expires January 1, 1898. Vote received, 29,270. Business, corner Niagara Street and West Avenue. Residence, No. 291 Porter Avenue. Telephones, "Amherst 27-A." and "Amherst 27-D."

MICHAEL J. BYRNE. — Term expires January 1, 1898. Vote received, 27,679. Business, No. 44 Builders' Exchange. Residence, No. 394 Fargo Avenue. Telephone, "Seneca 137."

A. FRANK GORSKI.—Term expires January 1, 1898. Vote received, 27,019. Business, No. 126 Townsend Street. Residence, same. Telephone, "Howard 258."

ANDREW J. KELLER.—Term expires January 1, 1898. Vote received, 30,750. Business, No. 757 Seneca Street. Residence same. Telephone, "Howard 168."

HENRY C. STEUL.—Term expires January 1, 1898. Vote received, 30,657. Business, No. 278 Johnson Street. Residence, No. 561 East Utica Street. Telephone, "Howard 175-Q."

CHARLES H. UTLEY.—Term expires January 1, 1900. Vote received, 24,044. Business, No. 82 Pearl Street. Residence, No. 263 Summer Street. Telephones, "Seneca 327" and Bryant 181."

HENRY ZIPP.—Term expires January 1, 1900. Vote received, 23,766. Business, No. 575 Exchange Street. Residence, No. 100 Walnut Street. Telephone, "Howard 187."

SESSION CHAMBER, BOARD OF COUNCILMEN.

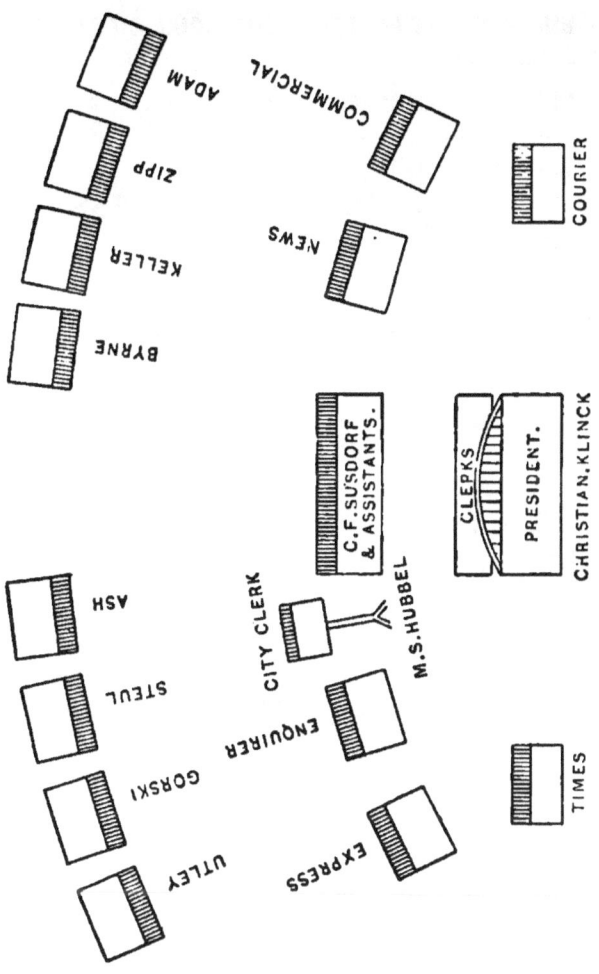

ADAM

ZIPP

KELLER

BYRNE

COMMERCIAL

NEWS

COURIER

ASH

STEUL

GORSKI

UTLEY

CITY CLERK

ENQUIRER

EXPRESS

C.F. SUSDORF & ASSISTANTS.

M.S. HUBBEL

CLERKS

PRESIDENT.

CHRISTIAN, KLINCK

TIMES

ORDER OF BUSINESS

OF THE

BOARD OF COUNCILMEN.

1897.

The business of all regular meetings of the board shall be transacted as far as practicable in the following order:

1. Roll call.

2. Reading, correcting and approving the journal of the last session.

3. Communications from the Mayor.

4. Reports and communications from corporation officers.

5. Miscellaneous communications.

6. Reading of, and action on, the proceedings of the Board of Aldermen.

7. Reports from committees.

Regular meetings of the Board of Councilmen shall be held in Room 28, City Hall, on Wednesday of each week, at 2.30 o'clock p. m.

NUMBER OF VOTES REQUIRED FOR VARIOUS MEASURES, ETC.

BOARD OF ALDERMEN.

Quorum 13
Two-thirds vote......................... 17
Three-fourths vote...................... 19

BOARD OF COUNCILMEN.

Quorum 6
Two-thirds vote......................... 6
Three-fourths vote...................... 7

COMMON COUNCIL.

Quorum { Aldermen 13
         { Councilmen 6
Two-thirds vote......................... 23
Three-fourths vote...................... 26

Auctioneers' Licenses—two-thirds.

Bonds—to authorize the issue of.
  Board of Aldermen.................... 17
  Board of Councilmen................. 6

Buildings, Frame—to erect, etc., unanimous in both boards.

Changing Name of Street—three-fourths.

Contracts—creating liability to be paid out of general fund, not to be ordered except on majority vote of both boards (elected).

Estimates—to alter or amend.

Board of Aldermen..................... 17
Board of Councilmen................. 6

Estimates—to adopt as altered or amended, majority vote.

Expenditures—in any department to increase upon certificate of Mayor, Comptroller and Treasurer—two-thirds.

Fines—to remit or to release from Penitentiary.

Board of Aldermen... 17
Board of Councilmen................. 6

Fish or Meat License.

Board of Aldermen.................... 17
Board of Councilmen................. 6
And after September 1st, in any year, unanimous vote.

Inflammable or Liquid Substance—to grant permission to manufacture — two-thirds present.

Lamp District—to order extended without petition.

Lands—determination to take.

Liabilities, to City—not to be released except by unanimous vote of all members elected.

Monthly Assessment Roll—to correct or revise—two-thirds vote in each board.

Ordinances—leave to offer by an Alderman—majority vote.

Pavements—to order without petition over $500.

Railroads, Steam or Street—permission to construct tracks.

Rescind or Repeal.

Rewards—to authorize Mayor to offer—two-thirds vote.

Rules—to suspend or amend.

Sewers, Sprinkling, Dredging, etc., to order on notice of intention or petition over $500.

Tax Sales—to redeem lands, or to rebate interest—unanimous vote in both boards.

Veto—To overrule on resolutions requiring majority vote.

Veto—to overrule on resolution requiring two-thirds or three-fourths vote.

Voting—to be excused from, in Board of Aldermen—two-thirds vote of those present.

CHARLES P. WOLTZ,
President of the Common Council

THE MAYORS OF BUFFALO.

From 1832 to the Present Time—A Roster of Distinguished Names.

1832—Ebenezer Johnson.
1833—Major A. Adams.
1834—Ebenezer Johnson.
1835—Hiram Pratt.
1836—Samuel Wilkeson.
1837—Josiah Trowbridge, M. D.*
1838—Ebenezer Walden.
1839—Hiram Pratt.
1840—Sheldon Thompson.**
1841—Isaac R. Harrington.
1842—George W. Clinton.
1843—Joseph G. Masten.
1844—William Ketchum.
1845—Joseph G. Masten.
1846—Solomon G. Haven.
1847—Elbridge G. Spaulding.
1848—Orlando Allen.
1849—Hiram Barton.

*Resigned December 22, 1837, and Pierre A. Baker elected.
**By Chapter 21, Laws 1840, Mayors of cities were made elective by the people, and Sheldon Thompson was the first one chosen for Buffalo.

1850—Henry K. Smith.
1851—James Wadsworth.
1852—Hiram Barton.
1853-55—Eli Cook.
1856-57—Frederick P. Stevens.
1858-59—Timothy T. Lockwood.
1860-61—Franklin A. Alberger.
1862-65—William G. Fargo.
1866-67—Chandler J. Wells.
1868-69—William F. Rogers.
1870-73—Alexander Brush.
1874-76—Louis P. Dayton.
1875-77—Philip Becker.
1878-79—Solomon Scheu.
1880-81—Alexander Brush.
1882—Grover Cleveland. *
1883—John B. Manning.
1884-85—Jonathan Scoville.
1886-89—Philip Becker.
1890-94—Charles F. Bishop.
1895-96-97—Edgar B. Jewett.

*Resigned, November 20, 1882, having been elected Governor of the State at the general election in November, 1882; Marcus M. Drake was appointed by the Common Council, Mayor, to fill the vacancy until a Mayor should be elected by the people; and the Common Council ordered a special election for that purpose, to be held January 9, 1883. On December 22, 1882, Mr. Drake resigned, to take effect December 29, 1882, and the Common Council elected Harmon S. Cutting, Mayor, to fill the vacancy thus occasioned. At the special election, held January 9, 1883, John B. Manning was elected Mayor for the unexpired term of Mayor Cleveland.

MARK SIBLEY HUBBELL
City Clerk, 1894-95-96-97.

THE CITY CLERKS OF BUFFALO.

Men Who Have Served the Municipality in This Capacity Since Its Incorporation.

1832—Dyre Tillinghast.
1833-34—Elijah J. Roberts.
1835—Theodotus Burwell.
1836—Elbridge G. Spaulding.
1837-39—Theodore C. Peters.
1840—Squire S. Case.
1841-44—John T. Lacy.
1845—Joseph Stringham.
1846—M. Cadwallader.
1847-49—Jesse Walker.
1850—Horatio Seymour, Jr.
1851—William L. G. Smith.
1852-55—Roswell L. Burrows.
1856-58—William H. Albro.
1859-60—Charles S. Macomber.
1861—Otis F. Presbry.
1862-66—Charles S. Macomber.
1867—J. D. Hoyt Chamberlain.
1868—Charles S. Macomber.
1869-70—George S. Wardwell.
1871—Thomas R. Clinton.

126   COMMON COUNCIL MANUAL.

1872-74—Walter C. Winship.
1875-76—Rensselaer D. Ford.
1877—Francis F. Fargo.
1878-80—William P. Burns.
1881—Francis F. Fargo.
1882-85—William P. Burns.
1886-89—William E. Delaney.
1890-93—Charles R. Marshall.
1894-95-96-97—Mark S. Hubbell.

MAYORS and CLERKS OF OTHER CITIES

FOR 1897.

CITY.	MAYOR.	CITY CLERK.
Baltimore	Alcarus Hooper	Chas. G. Leonard.
Binghamton	Geo. E. Green	Burr W. Mosher.
Boston	Josiah Quincy	
Brooklyn	Frederick Wurster	Joseph Benjamin.
Charleston	I Adger Smyth	W. W. Simons.
Chicago	Geo. B. Swift	J. R. B. Van Cleave.
Cincinnati	John A. Caldwell	Edwin Henderson.
Cleveland	Robert E. McKisson	Howard H. Burgess
Denver	Thos. S. McMurray	Denny H. Allen.
Detroit	W. C. Maybury	John A. Schmid.
Grand Rapids	Lathrop C. Stow	Frank D. Warren.
Hartford	Miles B. Preston	Henry F. Smith.
Indianapolis	Thos. Taggert	C. H. Stuckmeyer.
Kansas City	James M. Jones	Chas. S. Curry.
Lincoln	Frank A. Graham	John W. Bowen.
Memphis	W. L. Clapp	J. F. Walker.
Milwaukee	W. G Rauschenberger	Wm. E. Anderson.
Minneapolis	Robert Pratt	L. A. Lydiard.
Nashville	Wm. McCarthy	Sec'y to Board of Public Works, F. E. Kuhn.
Newark	James M. Seymour	Louis J. Wendell.
New Orleans	Walter H. Flower	
New York	Wm. L. Strong	Henry D. Purroy, County Clerk.
Olean	N. V. Van Franchot	Geo. H. Mayer.
Omaha	W. J. Broatch	Beecher Higby.
Oswego		Fred D. Wheeler.
Philadelphia	Chas. F. Warrick	None.

CITY.	MAYOR.	CITY CLERK.
Pittsburg	Henry P. Ford	Edward J. Martin.
Portland.	Sylvester Pennoyer	A. N. Gambell.
Providence	Edwin D. McGuinness	Wm. E. Clarke.
Richmond	Richard M. Taylor	Benj. T. August.
Rochester	Geo. E. Warner	Theodore S. Pulver.
St. Louis	Cyrus P. Walbridge	{ Henry Besch, City Register.
San Francisco	James D. Phelan	Wm. P. Sullivan, Jr.
St. Paul	Frank B. Doran	Mathias Jensen.
Syracuse	James K. McGuire	M. Z. Haven.
Toledo	Guy G. Major.	Lem. P. Harris.
Washington	The Commissioners of the District of Columbia—John W. Ross, President, George Truesdell, Major Charles F. Powell, Corps of Engineers, United States Army; Secretary, William Tindall.	
Worcester	Aug. B. R. Sprague	E. H. Towne.

A CHAPTER ON ASPHALT.—"Barber," "Standard" and Other.

Over 200 Miles of Smooth Pavement and What it has Done for Buffalo.

Buffalo is the best paved city in the world. It has over 200 miles of asphalt, or more than Paris and London put together. Smooth pavements in Buffalo are no longer an experiment. They have been tried here, and some are in a good state of preservation which have stood the wear of continuous traffic for over 18 years. The fewer interstices there are in a street surface, the fewer angles there will be where disease germs may lodge ; the smoother and more even the surface, the more readily it may be kept clean ; the nearer a city comes to achieving greatness with the least wear upon the nerves of its citizens, the more stable will be its growth and more comfortable its inhabitants.

The Barber Asphalt Paving Company has laid, altogether, 3,003,188 square yards in Buffalo ; The German Rock Company has laid

650,000 square yards of Barber asphalt; and the Standard Paving Company, organized in 1896, 4,791 square yards of Bituminous Rock, and 11,762 square yards of Trinidad, making a total asphalt surface in Buffalo of 3,669,741 square yards, many times more than the smooth pavements laid in any other city in the world, and these figures added to those representing asphalted streets paved by private capital bring the total far above the 200 limit in miles. Paving work in Buffalo is done by majority petition of property owners, whose preference in regard to material desired is always specified; but the Board of Public Works advertise for bids for all material for which specifications are on file in its office.

That asphalt pavement in Buffalo has proven an unqualified success is shown by the fact that Bryant street and Linwood Avenue, which were paved by the Barber Asphalt Paving Company in 1882, are still in excellent condition, having required very little repairs in the interim; Front avenue, North Pearl and Utica streets follow in 1883, and Ferry street—an excellent piece of work—in 1884. North Pearl street, paved in 1885, between Virginia and Allen streets, is as smooth as a billiard table and has had few, if any, repairs. And between

1882, when the first pavement was laid, and
1896, over 100 streets were paved by this company, including Main street, Whitney place,
Richmond avenue, Porter avenue and North
street; in fact, all the more prominent residence and business thoroughfares of the city.
The lesson of experience was well learned by
this Company, for in some of the earlier
pavement laid a tendency to roll, by the top
dressing, was discovered, which was obviated
later by the placing of what is known as a
"binder" between the cement on the foundation and the asphalt surface. This "binder,"
made of bitumen, tar and other compounds,
compactly welds the whole together, forming
a coherent and solid mass, which has with-
stood the severest usage. It has been well said
that the steam and street railways and the asphalt pavements have done more than any
other two agencies toward the development
of that Greater Buffalo, which is now an accomplished fact.

Asphalt pavement, as shown by this city's
experience, is clean, durable, noiseless, and
is fairly to be classified as one of the reasons
why the records in Buffalo's Bureau of Vital
Statistics prove that, while the city's population figures have been climbing upward with

giant strides, in inverse ratio those representing its death rate have gone down. This is because Buffalo is the best paved city, has the best sewerage system in the world, and because the purest water on the globe flows by in a resistless current, which is tapped by the water system of the city at a point far beyond the reach of possible contamination.

THE LARGEST HORSE MARKET.

Buffalo Leads the World in This Direction, and the Stock Farms of Erie County are World Famous.

Crandall & Co., of East Buffalo, who are among the largest horse dealers in the country, contribute this statement for the Manual:

"There is probably no one branch of business in the City of Buffalo that has grown to such vast proportions, in so short a time, as the Buffalo Horse Market. Ten years ago there was no market in the City of Buffalo for horses, except in a small retail way. The business now runs into millions annually, and the several firms doing business in East Buffalo handle over 40,000 a year. In the last two years a large export trade has been done, foreign dealers sending their buyers here to remain permanently, making shipments of from two to eight car loads per week.

"Horses are received and sold here, from all the Western States and Territories and from Canada, being one of the best distributing points in the United States, and the day is not far distant when Buffalo will be the principal horse market in America, as all grades and classes of horses are handled here.''

The year 1896, despite the competing interest of the bicycle and the use of electricity by street-railway systems, has been the greatest year in the experience of Buffalo as a horse market. The increase, during the past seven years, climbed steadily, each year showing a growth of 100 per cent. on an average over its predecessor, until now, at home or abroad, when a large purchase of horseflesh is contemplated, Buffalo is sought for as the best market in which the necessary choice may be secured.

Besides this, Erie county, of which Buffalo is the county seat, has more money invested in high-class horses than any other section of its size in this country ; its stock farms are famous the world over, and their output have achieved fame in many trotting contests. Within its boundaries are the famous Jewett and Hamlin farms, and others which have bred first-class trotting stock.

LOCATION OF PUBLIC SCHOOLS AND REGISTRATION AT EACH.

No.	Situation.	Ward.	Regis- tration.
High school, Court, corner Franklin		20	2,040
1—Seventh street, near Hudson		20	827
2—Terrace, near Genesee		19	385
3—Perry, near Illinois		1	709
4—Elk, near Louisiana		2	1,079
5—Seneca, corner Hydraulic		4	909
6—249 South Division street		3	913
7—Bailey avenue, corner Clinton		11	650
8—Utica, corner Masten		17	1,246
9—Bailey avenue, near Doat		18	959
10—Delaware, between Mohawk and Huron		20	757
11—Elm, near Clinton		6	676
12—Spruce, near Broadway		12	690
13—Oak, near Sycamore		6	652
14—Franklin, between Edward and Tupper		21	451
15—Oak, corner Burton		15	1,082
16—Delaware, near Bryant		24	921
17—Main, corner Delavan		24	1,032
18—School street, near Fargo ave		22	1,013
19—West avenue, corner Delavan		22	1,294
20—Amherst, corner East		25	847

136   COMMON COUNCIL MANUAL.

No.	Situation.	Ward.	Registration.
21—Hertel avenue, near Delaware		25	59
22—Main, near Erie Junction Ry. Crossing		25	162
23—Delavan, beyond Avenue "A"		18	221
24—Best, near Fillmore..........		18	2,531
25—Lewis, near William		11	551
26—Milton, near Seneca..........		5	957
27—Cazenovia, near Seneca.......		5	283
28—Abbott road, corner Triangle		5	360
29—White's Corners road, near Marilla...................		5	89
30—Hamburgh Turnpike, near Ganson		2	335
31—Emslie, near William........		9	3,150
32—Cedar, near Clinton		7	1,258
33—Elk, near Smith.............		5	898
34—Hamburgh, near Sandusky....		2	687
35—East Swan, near Spring......		3	859
36—Cottage, corner Norris........		21	549
37—Corner Carlton and Orange ..		16	1,419
38—Vermont and Hodge		23	1,008
39—High, near Jefferson........		18	1,368
40—Oneida street, cor. Fillmore..		10	879
41—Broadway, corner Spring		12	1,048
42—Corner Military road and Clay street................		25	575
43—Lovejoy and Gold		11	997

No.	Situation.	Ward.	Registration.
44—Broadway, near Peck........		11	2,042
45—Auburn avenue and Baynes .		24	1,234
46—Junction Edward and Virginia		21	466
47—Hickory, near Sycamore......		12	727
48—Edna Place, near Masten.....		17	849
49—Fargo, corner Vermont.......		23	799
School of Practice, Jersey, between Thirteenth and Fourteenth.		23	397
50—Eagle, near Madison		8	788
51—Hertel avenue and Gurnsey ..		25	850
52—Barry Place		24	1,127
53—Driving Park................		18	1,020
54—Parkside		25	480
55—Guilford street		14	1,552
56—Elmwood avenue		24	375
Kensington School, Richlawn and Shawnee avenues		25	76
Total...............			52,157

NEW SCHOOLS IN PROCESS OF CONSTRUCTION.

Masten Park High School, Masten street, between North and Best streets ; seating capacity, 1,000.

57—Sears, near Broadway.

58—Rother avenue, near Walden.

59—Glenwood avenue, near Fillmore.

60—Ontario street, near Saratoga.

Also new Buildings for Nos. 1, 12 and 18.

SCHOOL DISTRICT BOUNDARIES.

Statistics which will be found of interest to every parent sending children to Buffalo's Public Schools.

District. No. 1.

By Niagara River, Porter avenue, Prospect avenue and Georgia street.

District No. 2.

By Niagara River, Lake Erie, Georgia street, Court street, Terrace, Main street, Lloyd street and Buffalo Creek.

District No. 3.

By Buffalo Creek, Lloyd street, Main street, Exchange street ,Michigan street, South Michigan street and Lake Erie.

District No. 4.

By Michigan street, N. Y. C. Ry., L. S. & M. S. Ry., Elk, Hamburgh, Miami and Ohio streets.

District No. 5.

By Perry street, Buffalo Creek Ry., Clinton street, Fillmore avenue, Eagle street, N. Y.C. Ry. and L. S. & M. S. Ry.

District No. 6.

By Michigan street, North Division street, Cedar street, Swan street, South Cedar street, Louisiana street and N. Y. C. Ry.

District No. 7.

By W. N. Y. & P. Ry., N. Y., L. E. & W. Ry., City Line, Buffalo Creek, Seneca street and Bailey avenue.

District No. 8.

By Michigan, East Ferry, Jefferson and Northampton streets.

District No. 9.

By Broadway, City Line, Scajaquada Creek, N. Y. C. Belt Line, West Shore Ry. and Bailey avenue.

District No. 10.

By Main street, Terrace, Court street, Georgia street, Prospect avenue, Carolina street, Johnson Place, Delaware avenue and West Chippewa street.

District No. 11.

By Main street, Broadway, Michigan and Exchange streets.

District No. 12.

By William, Michigan, Genesee and Walnut streets.

District No. 13.

By Main street, East Tupper street, Michigan street and Broadway

District No. 14.

By North street, Main street, West Chippewa street, Delaware avenue, Johnson Place, Carolina street, West Tupper street, Delaware avenue, Virginia and Park streets.

District No. 15.

By Main, East North, Maple, Virginia, Locust, Cherry, Spruce, Genesee, Michigan and East Tupper streets.

District No. 16.

By Richmond, Lexington, Delaware avenues, Ferry, Michigan, Northampton, Main and North streets.

District No. 17.

By Delaware avenue, north line of Forest Lawn Cemetery, Humboldt Parkway, Puffer, Jefferson and Ferry streets.

District No. 18.

By Niagara River, Breckenridge, Grant, Sixteenth, Massachusetts avenue and a continuation of Massachusetts avenue.

District No. 19.

By Scajaquada Creek, De Witt street, Bird avenue, Herkimer street, Potomac avenue, Grant street, Breckenridge street and Black Rock Harbor.

District No. 20.

By N. Y. C. Ry., Austin street, Niagara River, Black Rock Harbor and Scajaquada Creek.

District No. 21.

By Colvin street, City Line, N. Y. C. Ry., N. Y. C. Belt line, Elmwood avenue, and the north line of the Park land.

District No. 22.

By Amherst street, Kensington avenue, City Line, Colvin street and N. Y. C. Belt Line.

District No. 23.

By Steele street, Kensington avenue, City Line, Scajaquada Creek and Humboldt Parkway.

District No. 24.

By Jefferson street, Northampton street, Humboldt Parkway, Scajaquada Creek, N. Y. C. Belt Line, Sycamore, Strauss, Genesee, Fox and Best streets.

District No. 25.

By Buffalo Creek Ry., Clinton, Metcalfe, Thomas streets, N. Y. C. Ry., Bailey avenue and N. Y., L. E. & W. Ry.

District No. 26.

By Buffalo Creek Ry., W. N. Y. & P. Ry., Bailey avenue, Seneca street, Buffalo Creek, Maurice street and Seneca street.

District No. 27.

By Buffalo Creek, Cazenovia Creek, Melrose street, Abbott's Corners Plank Road and City Line.

District No. 28.

By L. S. & M. S. Ry., Buffalo Creek and Cazenovia Creek, Melrose street, Abbott's Corners Plank Road, a direct continuation of Tifft street and Tifft street.

District No. 29.

By Lake Erie, Tifft street, and a direct continuation of center line of said street to Abbott's Corners Plank Road, Abbott's Corners Plank Road and City Line.

District No. 30.

By Louisiana, Sandusky, Vincennes, South, Alabama streets, Buffalo Creek, L. S. & M. S. Ry., Tifft street, Lake Erie, South Michigan, Ohio and Miama streets.

District No. 31.

By N. Y. C. Ry., William, Curtiss, Clark, Lovejoy, Shumway, Broadway, Johnson, Sycamore, Jefferson, Howard, Emslie and Clinton streets.

District No. 32.

By William, Spring, North Division and Michigan streets.

District No. 33.

By Perry street, Buffalo Creek Ry., Seneca street, Maurice street, Buffalo Creek and L. S. & M. S. Ry.

District No. 34.

By Miami, Hamburg, Elk streets, L. S. & M. S. Ry., Buffalo Creek, Alabama, South, Vincennes, Sandusky and Louisiana streets.

District No. 35.

By N. Y. C. Ry., Jefferson, North Division, Cedar, Swan, South Cedar and Louisiana streets.

District No. 36.

By Prospect avenue, Porter avenue, North, College and Maryland streets.

District No. 37.

By Maple, Virginia, Locust, Cherry, Mortimer, Genesee, Jefferson and North streets.

District No. 38.

By Normal avenue, York street, Porter avenue, Richmond avenue and Massachusetts street.

District No. 39.

By Sycamore, Jefferson, Best, Fox, Genesee and Johnson streets.

District No. 40.

By N. Y. C. Ry., Thomas, Metcalfe, Clinton streets, Fillmore avenue and Eagle street.

District No. 41.

By Broadway, Pratt, Sycamore, Jefferson, William and Walnut streets.

District No. 42.

By Scajaquada Creek, Elmwood avenue and N. Y. C. Belt Line.

District No. 43.

By N. Y., L. E. & W. Ry., City Line, Broadway and Bailey avenue.

District No. 44.

By N. Y. C. Ry., Bailey avenue, West Shore Ry., N. Y. C. Belt Line, Sycamore street, Mills street, Broadway, Clark, Curtiss and William streets.

District No. 45.

By Sixteenth street, Grant street, Potomac avenue, Richmond avenue and Massachusetts street.

District No. 46.

By Maryland, College, North, Park, Virginia streets, Delaware avenue, Tupper street, Carolina street and Prospect avenue.

District No. 47.

By Walnut street, Broadway, Pratt, Sycamore, Jefferson, Genesee, Mortimer, Cherry, Spruce and Genesee streets.

District No. 48.

By East North, Jefferson, Northampton and Main streets.

District No. 49.

By Niagara River, Porter avenue, Thirteenth and Massachusetts streets.

District No. 50.

By Spring, William, Jefferson, Howard, Emslie, Clinton streets, N. Y. C. Ry., Jefferson and North Division streets.

District No. 51.

N. Y. C. Ry., City Line, Niagara River, and Austin street.

District No. 52.

Scajaquada Creek, De Witt street, Bird avenue, Herkimer street, Potomac and Elmwood avenues.

District No. 53.

By Jefferson street, Puffer street, Humboldt Parkway, and Northampton street.

District No. 54.

By the north line of the Park land, Colvin street, N. Y. C. Belt Line, Amherst street, Kensington avenue, Steel street, Humboldt Parkway, north line of Forest Lawn Cemetery and Delaware avenue.

District No. 55.

By Lovejoy street, Shumway street, Broadway, Johnson, Genesee, Strauss, Sycamore Mills streets, Broadway and Clark street.

District No. 56.

By Lexington, Richmond, Potomac, Elm-wood avenues, the north of the Park land and Delaware avenue.

Districts 57 to 60, inclusive, are to relieve certain overcrowded schools, hence the boundaries cannot be given at this time.

FRAMING A CHARTER.

How the Present Excellent Code of Laws for the Government of Buffalo was Compiled.

Buffalo works under a revised City Charter, which became a law in 1892. It was the fruit of many public meetings, presided over by a committee of citizens representing the best of Buffalo's business, social and professional life, men prominent in trade, banking and other business, railroad men, artisans and representatives of the medical and legal professions, men conspicuous in mercantile pursuits, and members of the various labor organizations, all of whom had their share in the work, the committee holding open sessions, at which the various proposed enactments were discussed. These committees forming the main body of law-makers consisted of the following faithful workers:

Law and Park Departments and Harbor Master—P. P. Pratt, D. H. McMillan, John Esser, S. H. Cowles, James Mooney, T. Guilford Smith.

Police Justices, Salaries, Eminent Domain, Official Printing, Municipal Court, and General Provisions—Tracy C. Becker, J. C. Fullerton, E. H. Butler, Leroy S. Oatman, F. L. Beier, Henry Koons, Geo. A. Lewis.

THE MOST CENTRAL SHIPPING POINT IN THE COUNTRY.

Legislative and Executive Departments—R. R. Hefford, G. P. Sawyer, O. P. Letchworth, B. D. Rogers, George Sandrock, Geo. S. Wardwell.

Finances—Charles A. Sweet, C. M. Underhill, J. N. Adam, James G. Kerr, H. C. Harrower, W. H. Albro.

Assessments—John Fullerton, Henry Zink, Henry Spayth, Walter G. Shepard, H. J. Booth.

Police and Excise—R. K. Smither, Britain Holmes, A. H. Schlecht, A. W. Voltz, Gerhard Lang, Arthur D. Bissell.

Health and Charities—Dr. A. T. Bull, Dr. W. S. Tremaine, N. Rosenau, E. L. Cook, Dr. J. H. Pryor.

Fire and Water Departments—George Clinton, E. S. Hawley, John M. Welter, John N. Scatcherd, D. E. Newhall.

Public Instruction—C. O. Rano, J. M. Richmond, E. F. Latham, S. V. Parsons, W. G Gregory.

Election Department—Ward Officers and Their Duties—Norris Morey, W. H. Walker, G. N. Wattles, John S. Hertel, James Boland.

Public Buildings and Building Laws—John Feist, John Coleman, M. McNamara, C. B. Armstrong, G. J. Metzger, C. D. Bigelow, E. C. Hawks, Joseph H. Neil.

Engineering, Public Grounds, Streets, Water, Lights—John C. Graves, August Farren, John G. Milburn, Dr. Roswell Park, Harlow C. Palmer.

Revision and Compilation—R. R. Hefford, E. H. Movius, M. M. Drake, F. F. Fargo, R. F. Schelling, Geo. W. Patridge, D. H. McMillan.

Committee on Legislation—George Clinton, John G. Milburn, Tracy C. Becker, Ansley Wilcox, John C. Graves.

This public-spirited body of citizens held its sessions in the main committee rooms of the Board of Trade, and when its labors were concluded the instrument, as proposed, was acted upon and sent to Albany, where it was crystallized into the present law. Since 1892 there have been some amendments, tending generally toward improvement, but the bulk of the work of the Charter framers was well done and remains still intact.

The new Constitution of the State of New York, framed by the Constitutional Convention of 1894, did away with the admixture of State, national and local politics by so amending the Charter of the City that municipal officers must be chosen at separate elections, and providing for a two-year term of service of Aldermen after the inauguration of the new system, so framed, should have been completed. Under this it became necessary, in 1894, to elect all Aldermen for three-year terms; Aldermen elected in 1895 will serve two years, and an entirely new board will be elected in

1897, taking office on January 1, 1898, to serve two years each.

The Legislature amended the Charter so as to provide for the election of three Councilmen in 1895, to serve for four years, and it was also enacted ''that six Councilmen shall be elected in 1897, and they shall meet before the end of that year, at a time and place to be designated by the Mayor, and determine by lot, two of their number to hold office for two years and shall certify in writing to the City Clerk their determination. The term of office of the Councilmen elected in 1897, and so certified, shall be two years." At the annual election held in odd-numbered years thereafter, ''it is provided there shall be elected alternately five and four Councilmen for the term of four years," and the terms of other city officers also expire with the end of the odd-numbered years, successors to be elected the preceding fall.

And thus the machinery of the new Constitution has been perfected and set in motion, so that all city offices to become vacant will be filled by election in odd-numbered years; no municipal election occurring hereafter at the same time as elections for State or Federal offices.

LOCATION OF HOSPITALS.

Buffalo State Hospital, Forest Avenue, near Park Lake, Telephone, Bryant 262.

Buffalo General Hospital, 100 High Street, Telephone, Tupper 340.

Buffalo Homœopathic Hospital, Cottage and Maryland Streets, Telephone, Tupper 94.

Buffalo Hospital of the Sisters of Charity, 1883 Main Street, Telephone, Bryant 565-D.

Buffalo Women's Hospital, 191 Georgia Street, Telephone, Tupper 442.

Children's Hospital, 219 Bryant Street, Telephone, Bryant 29.

Emergency Hospital, Michigan and South Division Streets, Telephone, Seneca 338.

Erie County Hospital, 3399 Main Street, Telephone, Park 21-D.

Eye and Ear Infirmary, 673 Michigan Street, Telephone, Seneca 1253.

Fitch Accident Hospital, 165 Swan Street, Telephone, Seneca 300-A.

Lexington Heights Hospital, 173 Lexington Avenue, Telephone, Bryant 81.

Wilcox Private Hospital, 173 Lexington Avenue, Telephone, Bryant 81.

St. Francis Hospital, 337 Pine Street.

Riverside Hospital for Women, 306 Lafayette Avenue, Telephone, Bryant 595.

THE MECCA OF THE CONVENTIONS.

Ever Popular Buffalo, and How She Cares for Her Visitors—The G. A. R. Encampment.

Buffalo has come to be recognized of late years as the ideal convention city, for various important reasons, among which are its accessibility to delegates coming from all points in the Union; its location as the easternmost port of entry of the great lakes, enabling travelers from the West to reach it by that delightful mode of summer travel, the palatial lake steamers; its railroads, which gridiron and griddle it at every point, coming from everywhere; its cool evenings; its freedom from dust; its 200 miles of asphalt pavement; its varied excursion facilities, and its unsurpassed hotel accommodations for taking proper care of vast aggregations of humanity. These are a few of the reasons why Buffalo in the past two years has satisfactorily cared for more conventions than most other cities have since they were incorporated.

NO HEAT, NO DUST.

Probably nowhere on the face of the civilized globe is there a great city combining the climatic advantages of Buffalo, with so many other claims to popularity, as an ideal summer city. It is a matter of local proverb that "Buffalonians have no need to go away from home to escape the heat." Situated as it is upon grounds sloping upwards from the shores of Lake Erie, whose balmy breezes fan it ceaselessly, those terrors of less favored places, hot and consequently sleepless nights, often aggravated by the assiduous mosquito and his lantern-carrying friend, the fire-fly, are absolutely unknown. Whatever may have been the heat of the day, and 80 degrees is esteemed hot for Buffalo, sure as "the sun-set gun" booms over the waters of Fort Porter, the cooling winds of the lake sweep through the city, making its pleasant, evenings, and cool, sweet sleeps which follow them, summer experiences never to be forgotten by non-residents.

EXCURSIONS FOR VISITORS.

The boats of upwards of 20 lines of excursion steamers leave and arrive at Buffalo night and day through the summer season, from May until nearly November;

they ply to various ports on lake and river where summer resorts are established on the American and Canadian shores, and, including the wonderful rides down the river, the choice of two lines being given, to where the white surges of the Rapids and the wrath-like spray of Niagara Falls rises to Heaven like steam from the body of a giant in travil, even to those who have already seen that world's wonder, Niagara Falls, before, the new trolley lines connecting with the Buffalo steamboats on the American and Canadian sides, and running respectively to Lewiston and Queenstown along the very brink of the beautiful Niagara Gorge, afford an attraction and will yield a delight equaling, if not exceeding, that experienced on the first view of the cataract.

Niagara Falls and Buffalo are practically one city, but 30 minutes in time from each other, and connecting by trains on several roads, running at intervals on an average of half an hour apart.

UNRIVALED HOTEL FACILITIES.

Buffalo can take care of her guests in 1897, even though the Christian Endeavor Society and National Convention were to meet the same week.

In the matter of hotels of all sorts and
grades she can boast of more and better than
two-thirds of the cities double her size and
population in the United States.

All told there are 48 hotels in the City of
Buffalo, not all magnificent, but all comfortable, from the new and handsome Iroquois, the
famous Niagara, the Genesee, the New Tifft,
the old, but excellent, Mansion, that enormous
caravansary, the Continental, the Stafford, the
Broezel, and the Ontario, formerly Gruener's,
with facilities for accommodating respectively
from 500 to 1,000 guests, to the 40 odd others
of smaller capacity and lower figures. There
is not, of course, included in this list the
hundreds of boarding places and private
houses, which would on such occasions throw
wide their doors to welcome the strangers.
Besides this,

NIAGARA FALLS, OUR NEIGHBOR,

With its mammoth hotel establishments,
world-famous and luxurious, such as the International, the Cataract, the Hotel Kalten-
bach, the Porter, the Clifton and the Im-
perial, with several dozen smaller ones, is but
30 minutes' distant by rail and almost a
suburb of ''this City.''

One of the greatest conventions, numerically, which every year chooses an American city in which to meet, is the National Educational Association, which met in Buffalo in 1896, bringing a personnel of 15,000 people, as a conservative estimate, and she sent each and every visitor away deeply impressed with her hospitality and the ample means at her command for the entertainment of the stranger. In August, 1897, there will gather in this city the cohorts of the Grand Army of the Republic, and Buffalo will give it royal welcome and recognize its paramount claims to honor and pre-eminence and salute it and its members as worthy of all deference. Every year its membership decreases as the brigades, which answered to the call of duty on the fields of Appomatox, Bull Run and the Wilderness, and marched with Sherman to the sea, diminish in numbers as they reply to "boot and saddle," or the "reveille," which summons them to reply to roll-call in the phantom regiments of the hereafter.

Whatever doubts may have been entertained as to the ability of Buffalo to capably and hospitably care for the visitors within her gates was positively solved when the N. E. A. met here last year, and will be completely and

satisfactorily disposed of when the city shows
her ample resources to the 300,000 strangers
who will gather here in August.

Arrangements have been made for such an
entertainment of her guests, as will show that
the City is not only the most pre-eminently
progressive, but the most pre-eminently hospi-
table, municipality in America.

—

CONVENTIONS HELD IN 1896.

Church Clubs of the United States, Fourth
Annual Conference, February 6th.

The Master Painters' National Association
Convention, February 11th, 12th and 13th.

Supreme Council Royal Templars of Temperance, March 26th and 27th.

Homeopathic Medical Society of Western
New York, April 10th.

Eighth District Dental Society of New York
State, April 29th.

New York State Medical Association,
Fourth District Branch, May 12th.

American Ticket Brokers' Association, May
13th and 14th.

Rebekah Branch, I. O. O. F. State Convention, May 18th and 19th.

National Journeymen Horse Shoers' Association, May 18th, 19th and 20th.

Buffalo Alumni of the Ann Arbor University, May 29th.

Supreme Lodge Shield of Honor, 19th Annual Convention, June 2d, 3d and 4th.

Erie County Sunday School Association, June 2d to 11th.

New York District of the Evangelical Synod of North America, Annual Conference, June 5th to 8th.

New York State Association for the Protection of Fish and Game, June 8th.

Retail Butchers' Mutual Protective Association, State Convention, June 8th and 9th.

New York State Shoot, June 8th to 12th.

Presbyterian Missionary Congress of New York State, June 10th and 11th.

Supreme Lodge A. O. U. W., Annual Convention, June 16th to 30th.

New York State Pharmaceutical Association, June 23d.

International League of Press Clubs, June 23d to 27th.

American Association of Physicians and Surgeons, June 24th and 25th.

National Educational Association, July 3d to 12th.

National Association Saddlery, Hardware Dealers, July 14th to 16th.

International Cantonment Patriarch Militans I. O. O. F., Aug. 4th to 7th.

German Christian Endeavor Society, Annual Conference, Aug. 5th to 8th.

American Association for the Advancement of Science, Aug. 22d to Sept. 3d.

National Association of Stationary Engineers, Aug. 31th to Sept. 6th.

United States Veterinary Medical Association, Sept. 1st to 6th.

National Association Casket, Hardware Men, Sept. 9th.

American Public Health Association, Sept. 15th, 16th and 17th.

National Association of Builders, Sept. 14th to 22d.

National Association Commissioners and Inspectors of Buildings, Sept. 15th to 22d.

Democratic State Convention, Sept. 16th, 17th and 18th.

Polish Roman Catholic Congress, Sept. 20th to 25th.

Independent Polish Catholic Church Convention, Sept. 22d to 25th.

Annual Reunion of the Tenth New York Cavalry Veterans, Oct. 6th.

Federation of Women's Clubs and Societies of Western New York, First Meeting, Oct. 15th and 16th.

Royal Templars of Temperance, First Grand District Convention, Oct. 29th and 30th.

Epworth League, Buffalo District of the Genesee Conference, Oct. 29th, 30th and 31st.

German United Evangelical Synod of North America and German Reform Synod, Nov. 1st.

Federation of Women's Clubs and Societies, Second Annual Convention, Nov. 10th, 11th and 12th.

State Banking Association, Group 1, Nov. 19th.

CONVENTIONS FOR 1897.

National Brick Manufacturers' Association.

Junior Order of United American Mechanics.

The Buffalo Poultry Association.

National Association of Bridge and Structural Iron Workers.

Spiritualists.

Convention of Railroad Men, representing the Brotherhood of Locomotive Engineers, the

Brotherhood of Locomotive Firemen, the Order
of Railway Conductors, Order of Railway
Trainmen and Order of Telegraphers.

G. A. R. Encampment.

National Convention of the World's W. C.
T. U. and the Dominion W. C. T. U.

National Hardware Association.

Young People's Christian Union.

Baptist State Convention.

St. Andrew's Brotherhood.

Supreme Ruling of the Fraternal Mystic
Circle.

North American Bee Keepers' Association.

Great Council of Red Men of the State of
New York.

The Luther League of New York State.

CONVENTIONS FOR 1898.

The Packers of Canned Goods from the
Atlantic States.

The Machinery and Supplies Associations.

The National Foremen Cutters.

International Union of Bicycle Workers.

BUFFALO'S HOTELS.

Pourty-Eight Distinct Establishments Are Now Operating in the City of Buffalo Under City Licenses; the More Prominent of These and Their Convention Capacities Are Given Below.

Name of Hotel.	Capacity.
Iroquois	1,000
Niagara	400 to 450
Genesee	1,000
Tifft	850 to 950
Broezel	800 to 900
Mansion	800 to 900
Stafford	500
New Continental	900 to 1,000
Arlington	400 to 500
Ontario, formerly Gruener's	150 to 200

All of the hotels named above are large establishments, containing ample parlor room for ''headquarters'' of various delegations, and which could be used for this purpose if desired. And, of course, above are not enumerated the Niagara Falls hotels or the hundreds of boarding houses, and the many smaller hostleries, which have agreements with the local hotels to take care of their overflow of guests.

COMFORTABLE BUFFALO.

The Ideal Summer Climate of America—A Table of Temperature and Humidity which Explains Itself.

MAXIMUM OF WARM WAVE.

The following comparative table contains volumes of information about the hot weather, and shows that, with a comparatively moderate temperature, a brisk breeze and only a fair amount of humidity, Buffalo had the "best place in the procession" during the unusually hot summer of 1896.

	Maximum temperature.	Mean temperature day of maximum temperature.	Mean humidity day of Maximum temperature.	Wind movement day of maximum temperature.	No. of days maximum temperature exceeded Buffalo's maximum.	No. of days temperature reached 90 degrees or more.
Buffalo.......	85	76	66	307	....	....
Rochester. ..	92	81	77	175	10	8
Erie....	92	82	72	249	8	1
Cleveland....	93	82	83	285	8	5
Detroit	95	84	82	219	7	2
Chicago.	98	87	69	413	9	6
Cincinnati...	96	85	72	143	13	6
New York....	94	85	70	144	10	7
Philadelphia.	97	87	52	171	14	12
Baltimore ...	98	88	65	77	14	10
Milwaukee ..	98	86	74	325	8	6
St. Louis.....	100	91	66	320	16	12
Memphis	101	98	56	174	16	16
Pittsburgh...	94	84	70	109	11	5
Columbus....	94	82	84	157	12	7
Duluth.......	90	80	80	278	3	1
Albany.......	95	84	72	98	11	9
Kansas City..	103	90	48	246	16	11

THE MOST CENTRAL SHIPPING POINT IN THE COUNTRY.

SUMMARY OF HEATED TERM, 1896.

The following comparative table is a summary of the entire warm spell. It shows the mean temperature, humidity, velocity of wind, etc., for the 16 days in the various cities.

	Mean of Highest Temperature.	Mean of Mean Temperature.	Mean relative Humidity.	Mean Daily Measurement of Wind.
Buffalo...................	79.7	73	69	296
Rochester.......	84.6	75.4	72	161
Erie....................	81.5	74.6	78.5	210
Cleveland............. ..	84	75.1	81	239
Detroit.................	83.8	75.8	78 3	189
Chicago............... .	85.1	78.1	68.1	328

THE CAP JUST FITS.

An Outline of Chicago Fitted over Buffalo and Niagara
Falls Takes in Both and Shows the " Greater
Buffalo " of the Future.

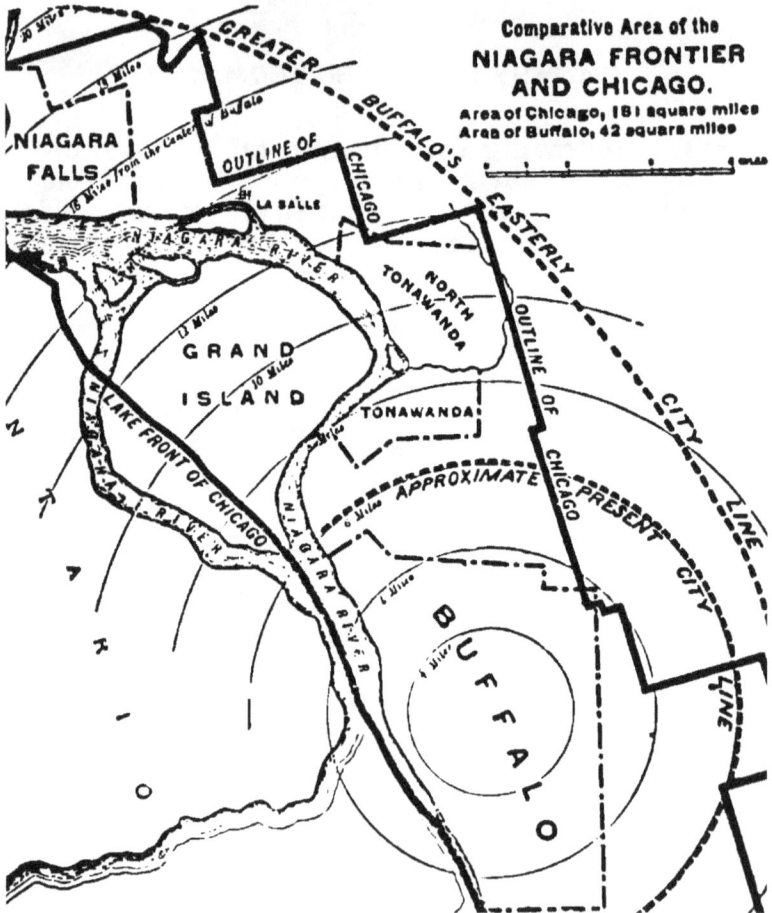

Comparative Area of the
**NIAGARA FRONTIER
AND CHICAGO.**
Area of Chicago, 181 square miles
Area of Buffalo, 42 square miles

NIAGARA FALLS

GREATER BUFFALO'S EASTERLY CITY LINE

OUTLINE OF CHICAGO

LA SALLE

NIAGARA RIVER

NORTH TONAWANDA

GRAND ISLAND

TONAWANDA

OUTLINE OF CHICAGO

LAKE FRONT OF CHICAGO

NIAGARA RIVER

APPROXIMATE PRESENT CITY LINE

BUFFALO

LAKE

BUFFALO THE ELECTRIC CITY.

Text of the franchise of the City of Buffalo to the several
companies for the introduction of electric power within
the corporate limits of the City of Buffalo. Adopted
by the Common Council, December 2, 1895:

First—Whenever either of said companies
shall desire to erect poles, string wires, or
cables, or lay conduits under this grant, it
shall file with the Board of Public Works a
plan drawn to scale, showing the streets, avenues, alleys or other public places, or parts
thereof, in which it proposes to erect poles,
string wires or cables, or lay conduits, and
the particular part thereof it proposes to
occupy for each such purpose, and shall at the
same time present and file with said board
definite written specifications of the electrical
conductors, wires, poles and conduits proposed
to be erected, strung or laid by it, specifying
the material and dimensions thereof, the
height of wires, the depth of conduits, the
methods of insulation and the devices to be
used for the protection of life and property,
which shall be the most approved, and said
company shall not have authority to proceed

with any of said work until the board shall have approved such plans and specifications as modified or amended and shall have reported its action to the Common Council, and said Council shall have approved thereof, and a written permit shall have been issued by said board therefor; and in addition thereto the consent of the Board of Park Commissioners shall be requisite as to any lands or grounds of which it has the general charge and control.

Second—All poles erected and conduits laid by said company, excepting lateral lines extending not more than 2,000 feet from a main line of transmission, shall be of sufficient size and capacity and of such construction as to afford suitable and sufficient facilities for at least one other company requiring as great facilities as the company receiving this grant shall at any time require in any such street, which additional space and facilities shall be shown and specified in the plans and specifications filed by said company under the first subdivision hereof and shall not be used by the company receiving this grant or its assignee or transferee, for a period of 10 years after its acceptance of this grant; and at any time during said 10 years said city may use such additional space or any part thereof for any public purpose from which it shall not derive a revenue without being liable to the company constructing the same for rental or other charges, and such use, if commenced, may be continued upon the same terms for the whole period of this grant. Said city may also use such additional space, or any part thereof, during said period of 10 years for the purpose of furnishing light, heat or power for other than public purposes, or may authorize any other company receiving a substantially similar grant from the Common Council to use such additional space and facilities, or any part thereof, for similar purposes, but in such case the City, or such other company, as the case may be, shall, before using such additional space or facilities, make compensation to the company receiving this grant, for the use thereof, which compensation shall be a just proportionate part of the cost of construction of the poles and conduits so proposed to be used by the City, or such other company, and of the expense of altering and repairing the same, together with six (6) per cent. interest upon such proportionate part from the time of the investment thereof by the company receiving this grant, and if City, or such other company, as the case may be, shall be unable to agree upon such compensation, the amount thereof shall be fixed by three arbitrators, one to be named by each of the interested parties and the third to be named by the two so selected, and their determination shall be final.

If the City or any other company shall commence the use of any part of such additional space or facilities, during said period of 10 years, as lastly above provided, such use as may be continued for the whole period of this grant upon the City, or such other company, as the case may be, paying to the company receiving this grant from time to time a just proportion of the cost of all necessary alterations and repairs to the poles and conduits so used, and if the interested parties are unable to agree thereto, the same shall be determined in the manner herein above provided for the determination of the compensation to be made in the first instance.

If after the expiration of said period of 10 years any of such additional space or facilities shall remain unused, and neither the City nor any other company shall have become entitled to use the same hereunder, then in such case the company receiving this grant may use such additional space or facilitis for its own purposes. If the company receiving this grant shall refuse to permit the City or any such other company or companies to use such poles and conduits as herein provided, or shall refuse to name such arbitrators, this grant shall thereupon become null and void.

The poles or conduits to be erected or constructed hereunder shall also be of sufficient additional capacity to accommodate six wires of the Buffalo Fire Alarm Telegraph and six wires of the Buffalo Police Signal Call System, and suitable and sufficient for such service, and the City shall be permitted to use the same without being charged therefor, and the space and facilities so provided shall always be held ready and available for use by the City.

Third—All work authorized and required by this grant shall be done by the company in a safe, thorough and workmanlike manner and under the supervision and subject to the approval of the Board of Public Works or such inspector or inspectors as it may appoint, and said Board may stop and prohibit the work, if not done pursuant to such plans and specifications and as required by it, and said board may at the expense of said company, at any time and without notice, do any and all work necessary to restore any street, avenue, alley or public grounds left by said company in a condition dangerous to life or property to a safe condition in said respects, and said company shall upon demand pay the city all costs of supervising such construction and of doing such work.

Fourth—That said company, upon reasonable notice from the Board of Public Works, shall at its own expense from time to time adopt and use such approved methods and devices and make such changes and alterations in its poles, wires, cables and conduits for the purpose of protecting life and property as the Board of Public Works may, with the approval of the Common Council, require, and in case of its failure so to do, said board may offer reasonable notice to said company, furnish the material and do the work necessary to that end, and said company shall upon demand pay the cost thereof to said City.

Fifth—The said company shall upon reasonable notice from the Board of Public Works, and at its own expense, raise or lower any wire or cable maintained by it and move any pole or conduit to permit the making of any necessary local improvement, or laying of sewer or water main or branch thereof, and on its failure to comply with such notice the said board may do the same, and said company shall on demand pay the cost thereof.

Sixth—The Common Council may at any time on the recommendation of the Board of Public Works require that the wires strung under this grant, or any part thereof, shall be placed under ground and the poles erected removed within such reasonable time as it may prescribe.

Seventh—Where said company shall desire to use a street in which a company having a franchise for similar purposes, containing similar conditions to those embodied in this grant shall have erected poles, strung wires or cables or laid conduits, the company receiving this grant shall use the poles or conduits of such other company, and make just compensation therefor as may be provided in the grant to such other company, or in other lawful manner, provided that such poles or conduits are suitable and sufficient for such use and that such use is consistent with safety to life and property.

Eighth—The said company shall, during the entire period of this grant, supply electricity to such extent as the capacity of its plant and its facilities for increasing the same will per-

mit to all persons and corporations desiring
the same in said city, and situate along any
of its main lines of transmission, or within
2,000 feet thereof, upon their complying with
such general rules and regulations not inconsistent herewith as it may make with respect
thereto, and shall not charge therefor a greater
proportionate price or higher rate per horse-
power than it shall charge other consumers in
said City for the same or a less quantity of
electricity supplied the same or a greater
distance from a distributing station and also
from a main line of transmission, and shall
not charge any customer a greater proportionate price, or higher rate per horse-power,
than it shall have previously charged him, or
a greater proportionate price, or higher rate
per horse-power, than it shall charge customers
at other points farther from its Niagara Falls
power-house for the same or a less quantity of
electricity supplied the same or a greater
distance from a distributing station. The distributing stations shall be shown by amended
plans, to be filed with the Board of Public
Works, before the company commences to supply electricity hereunder, and any line of
transmission more than 2,000 feet in length
shall be deemed a main line of transmission.

Whenever said company shall have received bona-fide applications for power aggregating one thousand horse-power, to be furnished within a radius of half a mile from any point in any part of the City where it has not constructed a line of transmission, and the applicants shall have tendered such company contracts for the use of power aggregating said amount for at least one year, accompanied by a bond for the performance of such contract, with two or more sureties with proper affidavits of justification, which contract shall conform to said company's general rules and regulations not inconsistent herewith, then and in such case the Common Council may order and direct that said company within six months thereafter extend its line of transmission and furnish electricity to such applicants in the manner and on the conditions hereinbefore provided, so far as the capacity of its plant and its facilities for increasing the same will permit.

Ninth—Said company shall annually, during the term of this grant, excluding the first six years from the date of its acceptance thereof, pay to the Treasurer of the City of Buffalo a sum of money equal to two and one-half ($2\frac{1}{2}$) per cent. of its gross receipts from all electri-

city sold or furnished for lighting, heating
or power purposes to any person, company or
corporation for use or to be used in said City
and regardless of whether such electricity shall
be furnished or delivered under this grant.
Such payment shall be made within 30
days after the expiration of each year from
the date of the acceptance of this grant, excluding the first six years thereafter, and
within every such 30 days the president
and treasurer of said company shall make a
verified report to the Comptroller of the gross
amount of its receipts for the preceding year,
and the books, records and contracts of said
company shall be open to inspection and examination by such Comptroller or his duly-
appointed agent for the purpose of ascertain-
ing the correctness of its report as to such
gross receipts.

Tenth—Said company shall be prepared to
supply 10,000 horse-power to consumers within
the City on or before June 1, 1897,* and it
shall submit the plans and specifications referred to in Section One for approval within 90
days after it accepts this grant. Said company
shall also be prepared to furnish ten thousand

---

* Time limit extended by Common Council until December 31, 1897.

(10,000) additional horse-power within each successive year thereafter for four years, as far as the demand therefor may require the same.

Eleventh—This grant is made for the period of 36 years from the date of this acceptance, as provided in the Fifteenth subdivision hereof, at the expiration of which period all rights and privileges hereby granted or conferred shall cease and terminate ; but at the expiration of 18 years from the date of such acceptance there shall be a readjustment of the percentages to be paid by said company to said City, such readjustment to be made by three arbitrators, one to be appointed by the company, one by the Mayor of said City, and the two so selected to appoint a third, and such arbitrators by a majority vote shall have full power to increase or decrease the percentages to be paid and to otherwise regulate or adjust the same as to them shall seem just and equitable, and their determination shall be final and binding upon both parties, and from the time of the filing of a written report by them with the City Clerk of said City said Section Nine hereof shall for the remaining 18 years of said term be deemed amended and modified in accordance with their determination.

Twelfth—This grant shall not be transfer-
able or assignable without the consent of the
Common Council, and said company shall not
consolidate or merge with any other company
or corporation or enter into any agreement to
prevent competition or to prevent the reduction of the price of electricity without such
consent, but the City of Buffalo, by its Common Council hereby agrees that it will, on
application of said company, to be made within six months after the acceptance of this
grant, consent that this grant may be assigned
or sublet once to a company organized
under the laws of this State for the purpose of
distributing electricity and operating under
this grant, and not having any similar grant,
or any other assignment of a similar grant
in said City, provided, however, that such
assignment shall not take effect until the assignee shall by a written communication to
the Common Council accept the assignment of
this grant and agree to be bound by all of its
terms and conditions and that it will pay the
same rate of percentage of its own gross receipts to said City and in the same manner as
its assignor company is hereby obliged to pay,
the intent being that the percentage shall be a
percentage of and determined by the receipts

of the assignee company, instead of the receipts of the assignor company. Such written
acceptance to contain a further condition that
if any other assignment or transfer of the
grant shall be made without the consent of
the Common Council the grant shall thereupon be and become null and void, nor shall
such assignment take effect until a bond in
the form and conditions provided in Section
Thirteen shall have been given by the assignee
and approved as therein provided, the form
and conditions of the bond to be suitably
modified to apply to such assignee, provided,
however, that the company may include this
grant in any mortgages which it may give to
secure its corporate bonds.

Thirteenth—Before any plans or specifications filed with the Board of Public Works as
herein provided shall be approved, said company shall file with the Comptroller a bond
to the City of Buffalo in the penal sum of two
hundred and fifty thousand (250,000) dollars,
with sufficient sureties to be approved by
the Mayor, conditional that no excavation or
obstruction will unnecessarily be made, placed
or continued by it in any street, avenue, alley
or public ground, and that all excavations
or obstructions made or placed by it at any

time in any street, avenue, alley or public
ground shall be properly guarded and the
public shall be suitably protected against accidents therefrom; and that any pavement,
sidewalk, curbstone, gutter, street, avenue,
alley or public ground torn up, displaced or
disturbed by it shall be replaced by it to its
former condition as far as practicable with all
due diligence, and that any pavement or sidewalk so removed and replaced shall be kept in
good order and repair by it for five years
thereafter; but it shall not be liable for repairs
rendered necessary by the acts of third parties;
and that it will fully indemnify and save the
City harmless from and against all claims,
actions or suits at law or in equity of any
name or nature for damages to persons or
property resulting from, occasioned by or
growing out of its omission to properly guard
any such excavation or obstruction or to
speedly remove all dirt, rubbish or other sur-
plus material placed or left in any street, avenue, alley or public ground or to properly or
speedily restore any street, avenue, alley or
public ground, which it shall disturb or inter-
fere with, to as good condition as the same
was before such disturbance or interference,
or in consequence of or growing out of the

making of this grant, or permitting the transmission of such electricity into the City, or
into the City in the manner herein provided,
and that it will indemnify and reimburse the
City and all other persons and corporations
for any damages or injuries caused or occasioned by it, its servants or agents, or the
electricity transmitted under this grant, to
any water, gas or sewer pipe, or any main or
branch thereof, or by any other structure or
improvement that may lawfully be in any
street, avenue, alley or public ground; and
that it will on demand pay all expenses of the
City in inspecting or supervising any work
done under this grant and in doing any work
where said company shall fail, omit, neglect or
refuse to do the same as herein provided, and,
generally, that it will well and truly keep,
observe and comply with each and every prop-
osition, stipulation and obligation of this
grant. The liability under such bond to con-
tinue until the filing in the office of the
Comptroller of a certificate from the Board of
Public Works that the terms thereof have
been fully complied with, and that such bond
shall be renewed by said company from time
to time as the Common Council may direct.
If this grant shall be assigned, as authorized

in the twelfth section, said company and its sureties on the bond given, as herein provided, shall thereby be released from liability thereon to the extent that the City shall be protected in the performance and fulfillment of its obligations under this grant by the bond given by its assignee as provided in said twelfth section and to no other or greater extent.

Fourteenth—If the said company shall willfully violate or fail to comply with any provision of this grant for 90 days after notice from the Board of Public Works, or shall willfully and unreasonably neglect or fail to comply with any notice given to said company under the provisions of the Fourth, Fifth or Sixth clauses of this grant, it shall forfeit all rights hereunder and this grant may be revoked and annulled by said Council.

Fifteenth—This grant shall not become operative until said company shall have filed with the City Clerk a written acceptance of all the terms and conditions thereof, and shall be void if such acceptance shall not be filed within one month after the adoption thereof.

Accepted by Power Company, Jan. 14, 1896.

CENTRAL TO EVERYWHERE.

Buffalo, the Headquarters of Cheap Power, is within a Night's Ride of Nearly Every Great City in the United States.

Half of the population of the Union lives within 450 miles of Buffalo, which is already the fourth commercial city in the world.

Draw a circle, with Buffalo as its center, and representing 450 miles in every direction, from center to circumference, and in that circle you will find located such great cities as Chicago, Detroit, Indianapolis, Cincinnati, Pittsburg and Toronto, to the northwest and southwest, and Washington, Baltimore, Philadelphia, New York, Jersey City, Brooklyn, Boston, Providence and intervening cities, to the south and east ; Quebec, Montreal and Portland, Maine, come also within the circumference. Within this charmed circle live 35,000,000 of the citizens of the United States, and within it are located 135 cities of over 20,000 inhabitants, the most distant of which is reachable from Buffalo in one short night's ride in a Pullman or Wagner sleeper.

This hub of half the Union, the greater manufacturing city than Manchester, the close rival of Liverpool, is only ranked as a commercial city by three others, according to the annual message of His Honor Mayor Edgar B. Jewett, who has made a study of this subject, and it has thus obtained a start in the municipal procession of the world which nothing can impede, retard or arrest.

BUFFALO'S POSITION

Among the Larger Cities of America in 1890 and 1895,
and the Population, Distance from New York,
and Difference Between Mean and
Standard Time in Each.

CITIES.	Population 1890.	Miles.	Hours.	Standard Time. * } Mean † } Time
New York, N. Y...	1,513,501	....	.... .	* 4 m.
Chicago, Ill........	1,098,576	912	24	* 9
Philadelphia, Pa...	1,044,894	90	2	† 1
Brooklyn, N. Y....	804,377	....	.....	* 4
St. Louis, Mo......	450,245	1065	29.40	† 1
Boston, Mass......	446,507	234	6	* 16
Baltimore, Md.....	433,547	188	4.09	† 6
San Francisco, Cal.	297,990	3209	132	* 22
Cincinnati, Ohio...	296,309	757	21.10	† 27
Cleveland, Ohio....	261,546	585	14.20	† 16
Buffalo, N. Y......	254,457	410	9 45	† 10

BUFFALO, 1897 389,138 7 YEARS' GROWTH, 140 543.

CITIES.	Population 1890.	Miles.	Hours.	Standard Time.
New Orleans, La...	241,995	1371	48	0
Pittsburgh, Pa.	238,473	444	12	† 20
Washington, D. C.	228,160	228	5.25	† 8
Detroit, Mich......	205,669	646	19.10	* 28
Milwaukee, Wis....	204,150	997	27.10	* 8
Newark, N. J......	181,518	10	.30	* 3
Minneapolis, Minn.	164,738	1332	50.50	† 12
Louisville, Ky	161,005	867	24.30	* 18
Omaha, Neb......	139,526	1402	43.30	† 14
Rochester, N. Y...	138,327	374	8.50	† 11
St. Paul, Minn.....	133,156	1322	50.30	† 12
Kansas City, Mo...	132,416	1385	41.30	† 19
Providence, R. I...	132,099	188	5.30	* 14
Denver, Col	126,186	1982	56.30	0
Indianapolis, Ind..	107,445	825	23	* 16
Albany, N. Y......	93,523	145	3.30	* 5
Columbus, Ohio...	90,398	540	17	* 28
Syracuse, N. Y....	87,877	293	7.15	† 5
Worcester, Mass...	84,536	190	5	* 13
Toledo, Ohio......	82,652	706	17.30	* 16
Richmond, Va.....	80,838	342	11.15	† 10
Nashville, Tenn....	76,309	1000	30.30	* 17
Memphis, Tenn....	64,586	1244	44.30	0
Grand Rapids, Mich	64,147	934	30.30	* 17
Lincoln, Neb......	55,491	1460	43	† 22
Charleston, S. C...	54,592	803	31	† 24
Hartford, Conn....	53,182	113	3	* 9
Des Moines, Iowa..	50,067	1270	41	† 14
Portland, Ore......	47,294	3232	133	† 20

BUFFALO'S CLUB LIFE.

The club life of a city tells its own story of that city's development and intellectuality; and clubs of the social sort with representative memberships indicate the possession of that wealth which is a pre-requisite to the leisure which makes culture possible.   The older and more wealthy a city, the greater the number of organizations of this character. They imply a great deal more than is usually understood, for through them is accomplished the amalgamation into a consistent and useful whole of many diverse characters and characteristics, which, standing apart and alone, would be far less capable of good to the community than when co-operating with others, so clubs have their beneficient   side and are important factors in the development of civilization.

On the tenth floor of the Ellicott Square Building, in the heart of the business district, occupying one-half of its space, is the home of the Ellicott Club—an organization of business men, primarily formed as a place of reunion for the midday meal, but which long ago outgrew the original intention of its charter members and became a place for evening rallyings as well.

There are 637 members in this club, and it is the handsomest business men's club in the United States. Its furnishings are incomparable, the decorations are of the Empire style, and its kitchen rivals in convenience, as its chef does in culinary genius, those of the greatest hotels in the world. The unique character of this club calls for its especial mention here.

The Buffalo Club is probably the oldest of the social organizations of the city, and its membership is in every respect highly representative of good citizenship and culture.

Other prominent clubs and their respective memberships are:

	No. of Members.	Telephone No.
Acacia Club, Masonic Temple............600		Seneca 406
Buffalo Club, 388 Delaware Avenue......500		Tupper 174
Buffalo Press Club, 208 Main Street......208		Seneca 723
Buffalo Chess and Whist Club, 584 Main Street........................98		None
Country Club, Elmwood Avenue, North of Park Lake.....................156		Bryant 44
Ellicott Club, Ellicott Square Building...637		Sen. 1567 D
Liberal Club, corner Delaware and Edward Street. (300 is the limit and there is a "waiting list.")..........300		Tupper 177D
Phœnix Club (Hebrew), 283 Franklin Street.......................116		" 147
Saturn Club, corner Delaware and Edward...............................271		" 177 D

	No. of Members.	Telephone No.
The Twentieth Century Club (Women), 597 Delaware....	280	Tupper 578
The University Club, 884 Main Street.....	246	" 247

Unique among the organizations is the last named but one, the Twentieth Century Club, on Delaware avenue, an organization owned and controlled by the ladies of Buffalo, to whose wisdom and good taste the city owes the classic structure the club occupies. It was built under the supervision of the following officers and directors: Miss Charlotte Mulligan, president; Mrs. A. P. Wright, first vice-president; Mrs. Henry T. French, second vice-president; Mrs. John C. Glenny, third vice-president; Mrs. Horace Reed, treasurer; Miss Mary Dudley, secretary; Mrs. Robert Keathing, assistant secretary; directors, Mrs. S. D. Cornell, Mrs. W. H. Gratwick, Mrs. E. S. Wheeler, Mrs. Robert Wilson, Mrs. Truman G. Avery, Mrs. E. L. Hedstrom, Mrs. F. L. A. Cady, Mrs. Carleton Sprague, Mrs. Charles Goodyear, Mrs. S. M. Clement, Mrs. Carleton Jewett, Mrs. H. C. Chard and Mrs. Ansley Wilcox.

The property, as it stands today, is valued at $75,000. The stock is nearly all owned by the club members, who receive six-per-cent. interest on the investment.

WALL STREET AND BUFFALO.

The Prices Paid for Buffalo City Securities Shows that they Lead the World as " Gilt-Edged " Investments.

Buffalo ranks with the highest in financial credit, as shown by recent sales of bonds. $555,000 School and Park 20-year-installment $3\frac{1}{2}$-per-cent. bonds sold February 5th, 1897, at an average of $1.75 premium on $100, and $194,687.11 Grade Crossing bonds, running 20 years and bearing $3\frac{1}{2}$-per-cent. interest, sold at an average of $2.27 premium per $100, and they do not contain the Gold clause, nor are they exempt from taxes.

The City of New York sold, November 9th, 1896, over $16,000,000 $3\frac{1}{2}$-per-cent. bonds to run 15 to 31 years at $10,471. These bonds contain the Gold clause and are exempt from taxation by the city.

The City of Brooklyn sold, November 5th, 1896, something over $2,000,000, and the highest bid was $10,110 on $750,000.

The City of Buffalo has not found it necessary to insert the Gold clause to find purchasers at a premium.

Boston bonds were sold November 23d, 1896, at $101,625 for $100.

Steadily through successive administrations the credit of the City of Buffalo enhances and its securities appreciate in value in the public mind and in the open markets and the exchanges. Actual sales made by the present Comptroller show a steady advantage in favor of the city, over those made by his predecessor, although that officer's record was a phenomenally good one and the prices obtained under his judicious management were greatly to the advantage of the taxpayers, but the present incumbent has done better yet : the former highest average price obtained for Buffalo City bonds was on an interest basis of 3.45, whereas, under the present Republican administration the interest basis has been but 3.33 ; all school bonds sold under the former were on an average rate of interest of $3.37\frac{1}{2}$, whereas a marked improvement in advantage has been obtained by lowering this price to $3.28\frac{1}{2}$. The tax loan bonds sold under similar circumstances during the Democratic administration, for 3.50 interest, and under the present administration for $3.33\frac{1}{2}$, all of which, while it may not demonstrate greater efficiency on the part of the present incumbent, or in any way reflect on the financial ability of his predecessor, proves, at least, one thing beyond demonstration, which is that Buffalo's position in the financial world is substantial, and that it is as the house in the Scriptures that was builded upon a rock, all of which is abundantly proven from without by this written testimony from Messrs. Roberts & Co., bond buyers of New York City, shortly after a recent sale:

"We have to again congratulate you upon having made a most successful bond sale. In view of the facts: That the City of Cleveland realized but $100 premium for their twenty-year per-cent. bonds, and that the highest bid received by the State of Massachusetts for its $27\frac{1}{2}$-year gold $3\frac{1}{2}$-per-cent. bonds was but par and 29-100, the sale of your thirty-year currency $3\frac{1}{2}$-per-cent. bonds, at a premium of $\frac{1}{2}$ per cent. is remarkable."

CENTRALIZING PUBLIC WORK.

The most distinct innovation effected by the new Charter was the creation of the Board of Public Works, which involved the centralization of patronage in the City of Buffalo, placing the reins of enormous power in the hands of three commissioners, constituting a central body of control. Subordinate to these commissioners, and holding office during their pleasure, are the heads of four departments of the City Government—now designated as ''Bureaux,'' the chiefs of three of which formerly derived their office directly from the people at general elections. These are the City Engineer's Department (now the Bureau of Engineering), the Street Commissioner's Department (now the Bureau of Streets), the Superintendent of Public Building (now the Bureau of Building), while the Water Commission has been transformed into a single-headed department or Bureau, governed by the Board of Public Works, which has its office in the City Hall. The three commissioners constituting this Board of

Public Works draw each $5,000 a year, and
their department is maintained at a cost to
the taxpayers of $10,388.16 every two weeks,
which includes the pay-roll accounts of the
central office and its auxiliary bureaux; the
salaries account of the main office, including
the pay of the Commissioners, amounts to
$20,900 per year.

THE BICYCLER'S PARADISE.

The Asphalted Streets of Buffalo in a Straight Line Would Cover Nearly Half the Distance to New York.

Buffalo has been aptly christened the "Paradise of Cyclists." With her 200 miles of asphalt pavement and 19 miles of park driveways, Buffalo is vastly better suited for the use of the bicycle for business and for pleasure than is any other city in the world. It is estimated, from the best information obtainable, that there are 60,000 bicycles in use in the city. The use of the bicycle for business purposes, especially for transportation from the home to the factory, shop or office, is extensive, and seems likely to be almost universal.

There are a great many near-by resorts and towns, to which on summer holidays many thousands of cyclists journey. The country roads in the vicinity are good, and will be better. Favorite runs in the evenings are to Tonawanda, on the brick boulevard, and around the Park system, and a cycle path to Niagara Falls is nearly assured. A trip to the beautiful South Park, with its botanic garden, is also becoming a favorite recreation.

The manufacture of bicycles and bicycle fittings are among our most active industries. There is an enormous investment in the business and the amount is largely increased this year. Employment is found for thousands of skilled workmen.

The municipal government in its different departments is prompt to recognize the rights of bicyclists, and accede to reasonable demands on their behalf, and if the Park Commissioners will kindly restrain the street sprinkler, in a measure, the ensuing season will be one of unequaled activity and enjoyment in the use of the bicycle.

Eight mounted bicycle policemen protect the rights of the wheelmen, drivers and pedestrians, and after a while even the Jehus of the Merchants' delivery wagons will be brought into subjection through frequent and judicious arrests and forced to abandon reckless and dangerous driving of their steeds, which has hitherto much imperilled human life, personal security and the pursuit of happiness.

DEPEW AND BUFFALO.

Fall River's loss is Buffalo's gain. One of the largest cotton mills in Fall River, Mass., has determined to move to Buffalo, or what is substantially Buffalo—the village of Depew, on the eastern outskirts of the big city and connected therewith by trolley. These mills employ between 350 and 400 hands, and Chauncey M. Depew is in this concern a heavy stockholder; many prominent Buffalonians are also interested in the new mills, and there will be no lack of energy or capital to keep them going and make them successful.

Lancaster & Depew Trolley. An electric-light system has just been established in the pretty suburb of Lancaster, and the superbly ballasted road running between Buffalo and that village will inaugurate, within a few days, a twenty-minute service between 7.00 A. M. and 11.00 P. M.

Buffalo's Business Exchanges: The Merchants' Exchange, the Builders' Exchange, the Lumber Exchange, the Live Stock Exchange, the Real Estate Exchange and the Board of Trade.

POLITICAL . . .

. . . INFORMATION

PERTAINING MAINLY TO THE

ELECTION DEPARTMENT

OF THE

CITY OF BUFFALO.

THE LAST ELECTION.

Votes Cast in 1896 for Important Offices, National, State and Municipal.

PRESIDENT.	United States.	Plurality.	State of New York.	Plurality.	Erie County.	Plurality.	City of Buffalo	Plurality.
McKinley	7,109,480	600,799	819,838	268,325	45,612	15,440	35,772	12,234
Bryan	6,508,681		551,513		30,172		23,538	

GOVERNOR.	State.	Plurality.	Erie County.	Plurality.	City of Buffalo	Plurality.
Black	787,516	212,992	41,585	8,186	32,004	5,383
Porter	574,524		33,399		26,621	

LIEUT. GOVERNOR.	State.	Plurality.	Erie County.	Plurality.	City of Buffalo	Plurality.
Woodruff	793,845	224,610	42,653	10,353	33,019	7,441
Schraub	569,235		32,300		25,578	

CONGRESS AND ASSEMBLY.

CONGRESS.		Votes received.	Plurality.
32d District.........	{ Mahany........ { Rung..........	18,623 14,765	3,858
33d District...	{ Alexander..... { Richardson....	27,573 14,503	13,070

ASSEMBLY.

1st District	{ McDonnell..... { Coughlin.......	5,615 5,691	76
2d District.........	{ Hill .... { O'Connor	10,407 3,557	6,850
3d District.........	{ Peevers........ { Maloney.. .. .	4,330 4,895	565
4th District........	{ Schneider ... { Mohring........	3,716 3,623	93
5th District........	{ Braun.......... { Streifler........	3.442 3,389	53
6th District........	{ Miller .... { McConnell. ...	6,258 3,793	2,465
7th District........	{ Steiner. .... { Veeder.........	4,618 3,036	1,582
8th District	{ Blasdell .... { Addington.....	4,941 3,772	1,169

THE CHEAPEST POWER IN THE WORLD IS AT BUFFALO

PRESIDENTIAL VOTE 1896, BY STATES.

STATES.	McKinley.	Bryan.	Palmer.	Levering.	Matchett.
Alabama	54,737	131,219	6,464	2,147	......
Arkansas	37,512	110,103	893	889	......
California	146,588	144,766	......	2,573	......
Colorado	26,271	161,269	......	1,717	160
Connecticut	110,297	56,740	4,336	1,809	1,223
Delaware	20,452	16,615	956	602	......
Georgia	60,101	94,232	2,708	......	......
Florida	11,369	32,213	1,778	868	......
Idaho	6,324	23,192	......	181	......
Illinois	607,130	466,703	6,390	9,796	1,147
Indiana	323,719	305,771	2,145	3,056	395
Iowa	289,293	223,741	4,519	3,102	453
Kansas	158,541	171,810	1,200	2,351	......
Kentucky	216,171	217,890	5,114	4,781	......
Louisiana	22,012	77,096	1,810	......	......
Maine	80,421	34,504	1,864	1,571	......
Maryland	136,978	104,745	2,507	5,028	588
Massachusetts	278,976	105,711	11,749	2,998	2,114
Michigan	293,327	237,251	6,930	4,968	......
Minnesota	193,501	139,626	3,202	4,343	867
Mississippi	4,730	63,457	1,021	390	......
Missouri	304,940	363,652	2,355	3,169	610

Montana	10,499	43,080	2,997	1,196	176
Nebraska	102,564	115,624			
Nevada	1,938	8,377			
New Hampshire	57,444	21,650	3,420	775	228
New Jersey	221,307	133,675	6,373	5,614	9,985
New York	819,888	551,513	18,972	16,075	17,731
North Carolina	155,222	174,488	578	635	
North Dakota	26,336	20,689		356	
Ohio	527,945	478,547	1,831	5,060	1,165
Oregon	48,711	46,739	974	919	
Pennsylvania	728,300	427,127	1,100	19,274	1,683
Rhode Island	37,487	14,459	1,166	1,160	558
South Carolina	9,313	58,801	824		
South Dakota	40,802	40,930		932	
Tennessee	148,773	168,176	1,951	3,098	
Texas	164,896	368,299	5,030	1,785	
Utah	13,461	67,053			
Vermont	50,991	10,607	1,329	728	115
Virginia	135,888	154,985	2,127	2,341	
Washington	39,163	51,646	1,668	968	
West Virginia	104,414	92,927	677	1,203	
Wisconsin	269,135	165,528	4,584	7,509	1,014
Wyoming	10,072	10,885		159	
	7,109,480	6,508,681	132,056	127,174	33,942

McKinley's plurality, 600,799.

THE CHEAPEST POWER IN THE WORLD IS AT BUFFALO.

OUR REPRESENTATIVES, STATE AND NATIONAL.

The Districts They Represent and the Boundaries Thereof.

CONGRESSIONAL DISTRICTS.

Rowland B. Mahany.

Thirty-second—1, 2, 3, 4, 5, 6, 7, 8, 9, 10, 11, 12, 13 14, 19 and 20 Wards.

D. S. Alexander.

Thirty-third—15, 16, 17, 18, 21, 22, 23, 24 and 25 Wards, and all towns of Erie County.

SENATORIAL DISTRICTS.

Charles Lamy.

Forty-seventh—1, 2, 3, 6, 15, 19, 20, 21, 22, 23 and 24 Wards.

Simon Seibert.

Forty-eighth—4, 5, 7, 8, 9, 10, 11, 12, 13, 14 and 16 Wards.

George A. Davis.

Forty-ninth—17, 18 and 25 Wards, and all towns in Erie County.

ASSEMBLY DISTRICTS.

Cornelius Coughlin.

First—1, 2, 3, 6, 19 and 20 Wards.

Henry W. Hill.

Second—15, 21, 22, 23 and 24 Wards.

Wm. Maloney.

Third—5, 11 and 14 Wards.

Wm. Schneider.

Fourth—4, 8, 9 and 10 Wards.

Charles Braun.

Fifth—7, 12, 13 and 16 Wards.

Nicholas J. Miller.

Sixth—17, 18 and 25 Wards.

Henry L. Steiner.

Seventh—The towns of Elma, Manilla, Cheektowaga, Lancaster, Alden, Newstead, Clarence, Amherst, Tonawanda and Grand Island.

Herman M. Blasdell.

Eighth.—The towns of Collins, Concord, Sardinia, North Collins, Brant, Eden, Evans, Boston, Colden, Holland, Wales, Aurora, East Hamburgh, Hamburgh and West Seneca.

ELECTIVE OFFICERS OF BUFFALO.

Public Servants Chosen Directly by the People, and Their Terms of Office.

OFFICE.	INCUMBENT.	TERM OF OFFICE.	TERM EXPIRES.
Aldermen..........	All members....	2 yrs.	Dec. 31, 1897
Councilman........	James N. Adam..	4 "	" " 1899*
"	James Ash......	4 "	" " 1897*
"	Michael J. Byrne	4 "	" " 1897*
"	A. Frank Gorski	4 "	" " 1897*
"	Andrew J. Keller	4 "	" " 1897*
"	Christian Klinck.	4 "	" " 1897*
"	Henry C. Steul..	4 "	" " 1897*
"	Chas. H. Utley...	4 "	" " 1899*
"	Henry Zipp.. ...	4 "	" " 1899*
Mayor..... ...	Edgar B. Jewett.	4 "	" " 1897
Comptroller........	Erastus C. Knight	4 "	" " 1897
Corp. Counsel......	Chas. L Feldman	4 "	" " 1897
Treasurer.........	Philip Gerst......	4 "	" " 1899
Supt. of Education	Henry P. Emerson	4 "	" " 1899
Com'r of Pub. Wks.	Chas. G. Pankow	4 "	" " 1897
Judge Munic'l Ct..	Chas. W. Hinson.	6 "	" " 1899
" " "	Louis Braunlein..	6 "	" " 1897
Overseer of Poor...	John Arnold.	4 "	" " 1897
Police Justice.....	Thos. S. King	4 "	" " 1899
Justice of the Peace	†Thomas Murphy	4 "	" " 1897
" " "	Thos. H. Rochford	4 "	" " 1899
" " "	Wallace C. Hill..	4 "	" " 1897
Assessor..........	Andrew Beasley.	6 "	" " 1897
"	Nicholas J. Mock	6 "	" " 1899
"	Albert H. Beyer.	6 "	" " 1899
"	Thos. F. Crowley	6 "	" " 1897
"	Edward G. Voltz	6 "	" " 1901
Supervisors........	All	2 "	" " 1897
Constables..... ...	All	2 "	" " 1897

Councilmen elected in 1897 shall determine by lot, two of their number to hold office for two years, and the others shall hold office for four years.

*See section 6 of the Revised City Charter.

†Vice John G. Miller, resigned.

THE BATTLE OF THE BALLOTS.

City and County Officers to be Chosen by the "People," in November, 1897.

Mayor, in place of Edgar B. Jewett.

Comptroller, in place of Erastus C. Knight.

Corporation Counsel, in place of Charles L. Feldman.

Commissioner of Public Works, in place of Charles G. Pankow.

Overseer of Poor, in place of John Arnold.

Assessor, in place of Andrew Beasley.

Assessor, in place of Thomas F. Crowley.

Judge of Municipal Court, in place of Louis Braunlein.

Councilman, in place of Christian Klinck.

Councilman, in place of James Ash.

Councilman, in place of Michael J. Byrne.

Councilman, in place of A. Frank Gorski.

Councilman, in place of Andrew J. Keller.

Councilman, in place of Henry C. Steul.

One Alderman in each of the 25 wards.

One Supervisor in each of the 25 wards.

One Constable in each of the 25 wards.

Justice of the Peace in 25th Ward, in place of Wallace C. Hill.

Justice of the Peace, in place of Thomas Murphy.

STATE AND COUNTY.

Assemblymen, one in each district.

Sheriff, in place of George H. Lamy.

One Coroner, in place of John R. Kenney.

County Clerk, in place of George Bingham.

County Treasurer, in place of George Baltz.

District Attorney, in place of Daniel J. Kenefick.

Superintendent of Poor, in place of Adam Rehm.

Keeper of Almshouse, in place of John G. Schlotzer.

Justice of Supreme Court, in place of Justice Childs.

Election Day, 1897, will be Tuesday, November 2d.

Days of Registration in 1897 will be as follows: First day, Friday, October 8th; Second day, Saturday, October 9th; Third day, Friday, October 15th; Fourth day, Saturday, October 16th.

Hours: 7 a. m. to 10 p. m., each day.

HEADS OF . . .

. . DEPARTMENTS

OF THE

CITY GOVERNMENT,

1897.

1897.

BUFFALO CITY OFFICERS.

EDGAR B. JEWETT,   **Mayor.**
Residence, 210 Summer Street.
Term expires January 1, 1898.

DEPARTMENT OF FINANCE.

Erastus C. Knight,   **Comptroller.**
Residence, 112 Bird Avenue.
Term expires January 1, 1898.

Philip Gerst,   **Treasurer.**
Residence, 1823 Niagara Street.
Term expires January 1, 1900.

DEPARTMENT OF LAW.

Charles L. Feldman, Corporation Counsel.
Residence, 159 Riley Street.
Term expires January 1, 1898.

DEPARTMENT OF PUBLIC WORKS.

Charles G. Pankow, President.
Elected Commissioner.
Residence, 289 William Street.
Term expires January 1, 1898.

Marcus M. Drake, Appointed Com.
Residence, 346 Bouck Avenue.
Term expires January 1, 1900.

Michael J. Healy, Appointed Com.
Residence, 215 Bird Avenue.
Term expires January 1, 1901.

BUREAU OF ENGINEERING.

Edward B. Guthrie, Chief Engineer.
Residence, 158 North Pearl Street.
Term of office, during pleasure of Department of Public Works.

BUREAU OF WATER.

Francis G. Ward, Superintendent.
Residence, 676 Seventh Street.
Term of office, during pleasure of Department of Public Works.

BUREAU OF STREETS.

Thomas F. Maloney,   Superintendent.

Residence, 923 Fillmore Avenue.

Term of office, during pleasure of Department of Public
Works.

BUREAU OF BUILDING.

John Reimann,   Superintendent.

Residence, 551 East Utica Street.

Term of office, during pleasure of Department of Public
Works.

DEPARTMENT OF HEALTH.

Ernest Wende, M. D., Health Commissioner.

Residence, 471 Delaware Avenue.

Term expires January 4, 1902.

DEPARTMENT OF PUBLIC INSTRUCTION.

Henry P. Emerson,

Superintendent of Education.

Residence, 122 College Street.

Term expires January 1, 1900.

POLICE COURT.

Thomas S. King,   **Police Justice.**
Residence, 109 Park Street.
Term expires January 1, 1900.

DEPARTMENT OF POOR.

John Arnold,   **Overseer of Poor.**
Residence, 1047 Ellicott Street.
Term expires January 1, 1898.

DEPARTMENT OF ASSESSMENT.

ASSESSORS.

Thomas F. Crowley,   **Chairman.**
Residence 582 Seventh Street.
Term expires January 1, 1898.

Andrew Beasley.
Residence, 16 Hayward Street.
Term expires January 1, 1898.

Nicholas J. Mock.
Residence, 291 Emslie Street.
Term expires January 1. 1900

Albert H. Beyer.

Residence, 532 Ellicott Street.
Term expires January 1, 1900.

Edward G. Volz.

Residence, 476 West Ferry Street.
Term expires January 1, 1902.

CITY CLERK.

Mark S. Hubbell.

Residence, 135 North Pearl Street.
Term expires first Monday in January, 1898.

FIRE COMMISSIONERS.

Jacob Davis,   Chairman.

Residence, 1320 Main Street.
Term expires June, 1898.

John F. Malone.

Residence, 169 College Street.
Term expires June, 1903.

W. S. Grattan.

Residence, 790 Ellicott Street.
Term expires June, 1902.

CLERK OF MARKETS.

Jacob M. Roesch.
> Residence, 613 Oak Street.
> Term of office, during pleasure of the Mayor.

DEPARTMENT OF POLICE.

BOARD OF POLICE, CITY OF BUFFALO.

Edgar B. Jewett, **Pres. ex=officio.**
> Residence, 210 Summer Street.
> Term expires January 1, 1898.

Charles A. Rupp, **Commissioner.**
> Residence, 47 East Utica Street.
> Term expires March 1, 1900.

James E. Curtiss, **Acting Commissioner.**
> Residence, 408 Richmond Avenue.
> Term expires March 1, 1899.

MUNICIPAL COURT JUDGES.

Charles W. Hinson.
> Residence, 172 Eagle Street.
> Term expires January 1, 1900.

Louis Braunlein.

Residence, 52 Orange Street.

Term expires January 1, 1898.

JUSTICES OF THE PEACE.

Thomas Murphy.

Residence, 478 Front Avenue.

Term expires December 31, 1897.

Thomas H. Rochford.

Residence, 266 Eagle Street.

Term expires December 31, 1899.

Wallace C. Hill, for the 25th Ward.

Residence, 2124 Niagara Street.

Term expires December 31, 1897.

SEALER OF WEIGHTS AND MEASURES.

Office at Police Headquarters.

Alfred H. Neal,   Chief.

Residence, 250 Normal Avenue.

Term of Office, during pleasure of Board of Police.

HARBOR MASTER.

Office, Ohio Street, near Main Street.

Robt. C. Soper.

Residence, 307 Highland Avenue.

Term of Office, two years. Term expires March 1, 1899.
Appointed by Mayor.

OIL INSPECTOR.

(Civil Service.)

Michael J. Noonan.

Residence, 156 Mackinaw Street.

EXAMINER OF STATIONARY ENGINEERS.

Office, Municipal Building, Room No. 22.

Fred C. Riester.

Residence, 152 Pine Street.

Term of office, during pleasure of Mayor.

INSPECTOR OF STEAM BOILERS.

Office, Municipal Building, Room No. 22.
George Reil.
Residence, 384 Madison Street.
Term of office, three years; expires April 12, 1898.
Appointed by the Mayor.

MEMBERS OF THE EXAMINING AND SUPERVISING BOARD OF PLUMBERS AND PLUMBING.

(Appointed by the Mayor.)

Office, Municpal Building, Room No. 1.

Samuel H. Wright.
Term of office expires December 31, 1899.

Jacob L. Mensch.
Term of office expires December 31, 1897.

Charles B. Huck
Term of office expires December 31, 1898.

OFFICERS AND EMPLOYÉS

OF THE

CITY OF BUFFALO.

1897.

MAYOR'S DEPARTMENT.

Mayor. SALARY.

Edgar B. Jewett $5,000

Secretary to Mayor.

Charles A. White.................. 2,000

License Clerk.

John G. Wilcox 1,200

Stenographer.

Jas. W. Murphy. 720

Detective and Messenger.

George B. Krug.................. 900

COMPTROLLER'S DEPARTMENT.

Comptroller.

Erastus C. Knight...............$4,000

Deputy.

Willis P. Fiske................... 2,000

Chief Bookkeeper.

Frank T. Moulton................ 1,600

Assistant Bookkeepers.

Edward H. Jones.................   900
Isaac R. Noble   900
George B. Curren.................   900

Statement and Warrant Clerks.

Edward D. Peters 1,100
Charles P. Lytle, Assistant....... 1,000
Albert G. Fellner, 2d Assistant....   900

Recording Clerk.

Frank F. Elliott.................   900

Market Accounts Clerk.

William W. Wallheiser   900

Countersigning Clerk.

Frank F. Walsh $800

Tax Sale Clerks.

Peter W. Taylor 1,500
F. J. Lesswing 1,000

Clerks of Arrears

Henry H. Matteson............... 1,000

Bond and Insurance Clerk.

John F. Diehl................... 900

Clerks.

Thomas Cassidy.................. 900
H. C. Fiske 800

Stenographer.

Thomas E. Kelly................ 720

AUDITOR'S DEPARTMENT.

Auditor (appointed by the Comptroller).

Anselm J. Smith................$2,000

Clerk.

David A. Seymour 1,100

TREASURER'S DEPARTMENT.

City Treasurer.

Philip Gerst......................$5,000

Deputy.

Charles H. Schwenk.............. 2,000

Cashier.

E. W. Seymour................... 1,500

Paying Teller.

Alfonso G. Feth................. 1,500
Henry J. Baker 1,500

Bookkeeper.

Eugene B. Penney 1,200

Assistant Bookkeeper.

William F. Pfeiffer.............. 1,000

Warrant Clerk.

Jacob Gerst, Jr 1,000

Clerks.

George Giess....................	$900
Frank Maischoss.................	900
E. J. Prouty....................	900
J. J. Donovan	900
William Roth	900

DEPARTMENT OF LAW.

Corporation Counsel.

Charles L. Feldman $5,000

City Attorney.

James L. Quackenbush 3,000

Assistant City Attorney

Edward R. O'Malley 2,500

Deputy Attorney.

Geo. P. Keating.................. 2,000

Managing Clerk.

Chas. F. Kingsley................ 1,400

Clerk.

Albert H. Jackson 1,200

Stenographers.

Miss Edith Sisson................ $900
Herbert C. Willet 900

Detective.

Jacob Springweiler............... 900

DEPARTMENT OF PUBLIC WORKS.

Commissioners.

Charles G. Pankow, Chairman $5,000
Marcus M. Drake................. 5,000
Michael J. Healy................ 5,000

Secretary.

R. G. Parsons....................$2,000

Assistant Secretary.

A. A. Thompson 1,500

Cashier.

J. C. W. Daly................... 1,500

Stenographer.

Isabel K. O'Connor 900

BUREAU OF ENGINEERING.

Chief Engineer.

Edward B. Guthrie............$3,000.00

Assistant Chief Engineer.

Harry T. Buttolph, per month... 208.33

Assistants.

Charles E. P. Babcock, per month 133.33
Charles F. Fell, per month 133.33
Alexander W. Hoffman, per month 133.33
George H. Norton, per month 133.33
F. V. E. Bardol, per month 133.33
H. J. March, per month.......... 133.33
Charles H. Tutton, per month.... 133.33

Levelers.

George T. Roberts, per month.... 100.00
L. H. Rathman, per month....... 100.00
L. W. Eighmy, per month........ 100.00
Louis Leitze, per month.... ..... 100.00
Joseph Ditto, per month.......... 100.00
J. A. Vandewater, per month 100.00
Jerry Donavan, per month........ 100.00

Superintendent of Street Work.

Daniel Collins, Sup't St. Rep'rs..$1,500.00

Clerks.

John A. Bodamer(chief),per month 125.00
Wm. Messing, per month......... 83.33
Charles A. Perry, per month...... 83.33

Sidewalk Clerk.

William O. Peck, per month...... 100.00

Stenographer.

J. M. Alexandre................. 900.00

Draughtsman

F. J. Tresise, per month......... 80.00

Rod and Axe Men.

Sixteen, each per month......... 75.00

General Inspector.

O. F. Whitford, per month 100.00

Inspectors of House Connections.

Jacob Hager, per diem........... 3.00
J. J. Purcell, per diem.......... 3.00

Inspector of General Repairs.

William Meyers, per diem $3.00

Keeper of Inlets.

Edward Rowland, per month 50.00

Inspector of Dredging.

Wm. Cochrane, per diem 3.00

BUREAU OF WATER.

Office, Municipal Building.

Superintendent.

Francis G. Ward $3,000
Louis H. Knapp, Assistant Supt.
 and Engineer................ 2,500
A. G. Frankenstein, Registrar 1,500
A. W. Guild, Cashier............. 1,200
Jas. G. Harrington, Asst. Cashier. 1,000
W. Bruner, Bookkeeper........... 1,000

Clerks.

Stanley E. Curtin $900
Frank S. Smith 900
J. W. Messing 900
Thos. W. Bishop 900
Max Geiger. 900
W. D. Fitzpatrick 900
A. E. Oehler 900
16 Inspectors, per month 65

Storehouse.

C. E. Richardson, Foreman of Repairs 1,500
M. M. Hollenbeck, Foreman of Extensions. 1,000
G. H. Chambers, Storekeeper...... 900
George Schneider, Plumber, per month 80
John Collins, Plumber's helper, per month 45
Herman W. Lindeke, Carpenter, per month 65
Wm. Gorski, Carpenter's helper, per month.................... 45
Henry Layer, Foreman of Stables, per month.................... 65
Bernard Zittrell, Stableman........ 45
M. Lynett, Teamster, per month .. 50

Storehouse—*Continued.*

John Fisher, Watchman, per month	$50
H. Zurbrick, Blacksmith, per month	65
John Meissner, Blacksmith's helper	40
J. Fisher, Teamster, per day	2
George Wasmuth, Tapper, per month	70
E. Silvey, Tapper, per month......	70
George Haeffner, Ass't Tapper.....	45
Wm. Connolly, Ass't Tapper	45
Foreman of Leaks, per month......	75
Foreman of Valves, per month	65
Foreman of Hydrants, per month..	65
23 Repairers, per month	55
One Laborer at Storehouse, per month........................	50

Pumping Station.

Patrick Brennan, Chief Engineer	$2,000.00
One Clerk to Engineer..........	720.00
Nine Engineers, each...........	1,050.00
Six Firemen, per day..........	2.25
24 Firemen, per day...........	2.00
One Oiler, per day.............	2.00
Five Oilers, etc., per day.......	1.50
10 Wipers, per month..........	40.00
Four Boiler-cleaners, per month	40.00
Two Machinists, per day........	2.50
Two Machinists' helpers, per month.....................	40.00

Pumping Station.—*Continued.*

One Carpenter, per month	$65.00
One Carpenter's helper, per month	45.00
Three Reservoir Keepers, per month	45.00
Two Keepers, Inlet Pier, per month	50.00

BUREAU OF STREETS.

Superintendent.

Thomas F. Maloney $3,000.00

First Assistant and Acting Supt.

L. J. Baitz, per month 125.00

Second Assistant Superintendent.

Samuel Wolffsohn, per month.... 85.00

Clerks.

R. H. Parsons, Chief, per month	100.00
Joseph D. Hanrahan, per month	75.00
Daniel E. Mahoney.............	75.00
John Riley	75.00
Henry H. Edson....	900.00

Stenographer.

Josephine A. Hanavan, per month 75.00

General Inspector.

Wm. Henderson, per month $83.33

Inspectors of Lamps.

E. H. Sigison, per month....... 83.33

Street and Health Inspectors.

John Barry, per month......... 65.00
R. J. Burchfield, per month 65.00
Henry A. Miller, per month 65.00
John N. Snyder, per month 65.00
Timothy Clifford, per month.... 65.00
Benj. F. Van Ame, per month.. 65.00
Thomas Burton, per month 65.00
John F. Dreger, per month 65.00
George W. Ebbs, per month 65.00
John Devine, per month........ 65.00
M. F. Hutchinson, per month .. 65.00
John Shalloe, per month........ 65.00
Rufus T. Byrne, per month..... 65.00

BUREAU OF BUILDING.

Superintendent.

John Reimann $3,000.00

Assistant Superintendent.
John Kirchgasser..............$1,500.00
Chief Clerk.
Thad. W. Gardiner............ 1,200.00
Permit Clerk.
Ellsworth N. Croll............. 900.00
Registrar.
Henry W. Nachbar 1,200.00
Inspectors.
Howard L. Beck................ 1,000.00
Albert C. Wunsch 1,000.00
F. C. Bergholz 1,000.00
Thomas F. Carmody........... 1,000.00
John J. Kavany............... 1,000.00
Wm. F. Meyer (coal), per diem   3.00
Structural Engineer.
Wm. G. Houck. 1,500.00

MUNICIPAL BUILDING.

Janitors.
John F. Townsend, per month. ...$83.33
Engineer (one), per month 75.00
Fireman (one,) per month......... 58.33

Janitors.—*Continued.*

Porters (two) each, per month.....$50.00
Night watchman (one), per month. 62.50
Elevator Conductor (one),per month 35.42
Scrub Women (eight), each, per day 1.00

BOARD OF HEALTH.

The Mayor, Edgar B. Jewett (ex-officio).

Charles G. Pankow, President Department of Public Works.

Ernest Wende, M. D., Health Commissioner, Chairman.

August Schneider, Secretary.

DEPARTMENT OF HEALTH.

Health Commissioner.

Ernest Wende, M. D..............$4,000

Assistant Health Officer.

Walter D. Greene, M. D.......... 2,000

Clerk Department of Health.

August Schneider.................$1,500

Registrar Vital Statistics.

Franklin C. Gram, M. D......... 1,200

Clerks.

Charles Diebold, Jr............... 900
Leon S. Barnard 900

Stenographer and Clerk.

Stephen W. Bateson 900

City Chemist.

Herbert M. Hill, M.D............. 1,000

Inspector Food and Supplies and Drugs.

W. H. Heath, M. D............... 1,000

Bacteriologist.

William G. Bissell, M. D......... 1,500

Assistant Bacteriologist.

Thomas B. Carpenter.......... 1,200

Tenement and Lodging House Inspector.

D. J. Constantine, M. D 1,000

Sanitary Inspectors.

James D. Wood $1,000
J. W. Van Peyma 1,000
Joseph H. Carley 1.000
Frederick B. Willard, M. D 1,000
Frank B. Smering 1,000

Inspector of Plumbing and Drainage.

Dean Wilson 1,400

Assistant Inspectors Plumbing and Drainage.

John J. Boyne 1,200
William H. White 1,200
John McGorey 1,200
Charles S. Webster 1,200
Peter J. Lynch 1,200

Cattle Inspector.

John Rast 1,500

Assistant Cattle Inspector.

Henry A. Munzert 1,000

City Scavenger.

Philip Buettner 900

Keeper Quarantine Hospital
      A. T. O'Hara, M. D............$1,200.00
Fumigating and Placarding.
      Charles Rittling, per day........   2.50
City Physicians.
      George F. Cott, M.D..1st District 500.00
      D. W. C. Greene, M.D.2d   "   400.00
      A. W. Bayliss,M. D...3d   "   400.00
      G. W. Lewis, Jr.,M.D.4th   "   450.00
      H. G. Bentz, M.D.....5th   "   400.00
      William Hoddick,M.D.6th   "   400.00
      E. C. Waldurff, M.D...7th   "   400.00
      J. A. Hoffmeyer, M.D..8th   "   250.00
      E. A. Fisher, M. D., Homœo-
         pathic, East Side Main Street 200.00
      Geo. R. Stearus, M.D., Homœo-
         pathic, West Side Main Street 200.00

DEPARTMENT OF PUBLIC INSTRUCTION.

School Examiners. (Office in Austin
      Building, corner of Eagle and
      Franklin Streets. Appointed
      by the Mayor.)
      Henry Altman $500
            Term expires February 3, 1901.
      Conrad Diehl................. $500
            Term expires February 3, 1902.

School Examiners—*Continued.*

Lilly Lord Tifft $500
Term expires February 3, 1900.
Timothy J. Mahoney 500
Term expires February 3, 1899.
Seward A. Simons 500
Term expires February 3, 1898.
Chas. C. Morey, Secretary 1,200

Superintendent of Education.

Henry P. Emerson 5,000

Secretary and Superintendent of German.

Matthew J. Chemnitz 2,500

Clerks.

William J. Strong 1,400
William J. Burke 1,200
William M. Mumm, Stenographer 900

Attendance Officers.

Central District—Chas. F. Reif .. 850
S. E. District—Louis Trost 850
S. W. District—Ralph Courter ... 850
N. E. District—Robert F. Wegener 850
N. W. District—Alfred Brener ... 850

Teachers.

One 2,500
Three, each 2,000
One 1,800
Twenty-eight, each 1,600

Teachers—*Continued.*

Two, each $1,550
Fifteen, each..................... 1,500
Seven, each 1,400
Four, each 1,300
One 1,250
Four, each........................ 1,200
One 1,100
Five, each........................ 1,000
One   950
Three, each.......................   900
Nine, each........................   850
Six, each.........................   800
Eleven, each......................   750
Sixty-two, each   700
Five, each   650
Six hundred and forty-three, each.   600
Two hundred and seventy-eight,
    each.......................$400 to 600

Janitors.

One $1,700
One 1,500
Two, each..................... 1,300
One 1,250
Two, each..................... 1,200
One 1,100
One 1,075
Two, each..................... 1,050

Janitors—*Continued.*

Three, each	$1,000
Five, each	950
Three, each	900
Two, each	850
Six, each	800
Two, each	750
Three, each	700
Two, each	650
Two, each	600
One	550
Five, each	500
Three, each	400
Three, each	350
Three, each	300
Three, each	250
One	225
One	220
Thirteen, each	200
One	192
One	175
One	170
Seven, each	150
One	125
One	120
One	108
Seven, each	100
Two, each	50

DEPARTMENT OF POOR.

Overseer.

    John Arnold............ ....$3,500

Deputy.

    L. J. Kenngott...... 1,500

Clerks.

    John Dietzer... 900
    Charles McBean................. 900
    John J. Aeschbach 900
    Charles J. Baker 900

Janitress.

    Clara Gardner.................. 200

DEPARTMENT OF ASSESSMENT.

Assessors.

    Thomas F. Crowley (Chairman) . .$3,500
    Albert H. Beyer (Secretary) 3,500
    Andrew Beasley..   3,500
    Nicholas J. Mock.   3,500
    Edward G. Volz..   3,500

Clerks.

Joseph Mayer (Chief)	$1,500
Charles H. Scheu	1,000
Geo. A. Halbin (Draughtsman)	960
Matthew Ludwig	900
Philip J. Stalter	900
Clark N. Leonard	900
Daniel F. Manley	900
Charles Gaetz, Jr.	900
Daniel P. Murphy	900
Henry G. Sauter	900
John Volz	900
J. H. Short	900

CITY CLERK'S DEPARTMENT.

City Clerk.

Mark S. Hubbell	$2,500

Deputy.

Charles F. Susdorf	2,000

Chief Clerk.

Alexander Kirsch	1,500

Warrant Clerk.

C. J. Fitzpatrick	1,200

Assistant Warrant Clerk.

John Johnston $1,000

General Clerk.

Charles F. Stillman.............. 1,000

Index Clerk.

Charles O. Backman.............. 900

Clerk.

Frank H. La Montagne............ 900

DEPARTMENT OF FIRE.

Commissioners.

Jacob Davis, Chairman, per session $5.00
Wm. N. Smith, per session... 5.00
Wm. S. Grattan, per session 5.00
John Weiss, Secretary.... 1,500
E. C. O'Brien, Surgeon .. 1,500

Chief of Department.

Bernard J. McConnell...... 3,000

Assistant Chief of Department.

Edward P. Murphy........ 2,200

Battalion Chiefs.

Five, each........................ 1,600

Headquarters Staff.

One Master Mechanic $1,500
One Chief Operator............... 1,800
Three Operators, each............ 1,100
One Line Repairer 1,100
Two Linemen, each 900
One Superintendent of Horses 1,400

Captains.

Thirty-eight, each................. 1,100

Lieutenants.

Forty, each....................... 950

Engineers.

Thirty-one, each 1,000

Firemen, First Grade.

Two hundred and twenty-five, each 900

Firemen, Second Grade.

Thirty-eight, each................. 800
Pilots, Fire Boat, four, each....... 1,100

Substitutes.

Thirty-nine, each 600

DEPARTMENT OF POLICE.

BOARD OF POLICE.

Commissioners.

Edgar B. Jewett (Ex-officio) $500
James E. Curtiss, Acting Com'r... 2,500
Charles A. Rupp 2,500

Superintendent.

W. S. Bull........................ 3,500

Assistant Superintendent.

Patrick V. Cusack................. 2,500

Clerk Board of Police.

Charles O. Hertel. 1,200

Stenographer.

Charles E. Knowles............... 1,000

Surgeon.

Joseph Fowler.................... 1,500

Superintendent of Electrical Department.

Thomas J. Welch............. .   1,500

Clerk to Superintendent of Police.

Frank V. Parsons 1,200

Chief Clerk and Operator.

Thomas O'Brian $1,400

Assistant Clerk and Operator.

George A. Schmidt............... 1,000

Detectives.

Fifteen, each..................... 1,200

Captains.

Thirteen, each 1,400

Precinct Specials.

Twenty-six, each................. 1,000

Sergeants.

Thirty-nine, each 950

Doormen.

Thirty-nine, each 900

Operators Patrol Signal System.

Eight, each 900

Patrolmen.

Three hundred and thirty-nine,
    each 900
Ninety, each 800
Thirty-seven, each 720
One Conductor of Prison Van...... 950
One Conductor of Prison Van...... 900

Hostlers.

Six, each........... $720

Janitress.

One....... 1,800

Janitresses.

Two, each 360
Three, each 400
One 450
Six, each........................ 500

Drivers of Patrol Wagons.

Twenty-four, each................ 900

SEALERS OF WEIGHTS AND MEASURES.

Chief.

Alfred H. Neal................... $2,000

Assistants.

Charles Henafelt 1,000
Adolf Karl....... 1,000

Engineers.

Two, each........................ 900

Matrons.

Three, each 600

Watchman.

One $540

Interpreter Police Court.

One 900

Linemen.

Three, each. 720

Batteryman.

One 540

Laborer.

One 540

JUDICIARY DEPARTMENT.

MUNICIPAL COURT JUDGES.

Charles W. Hinson. $4,000
Louis Braunlein. 4,000

Clerk.

Harry C. Green. 1,300

Deputy.

Charles H. Gosrow. 1,100

Special Deputies.

Thomas W. Nisell	$900
Warren F. Hedstrom	900
Richard F. Coughlin	900

Stenographers.

Frederick Denny	1,200
Edwin E. Webb	1,200

POLICE COURT.

Justice.

Thomas S. King	$5,000

Clerk.

Charles B. Sherwood	1,200

Deposition Clerk.

Alfred C. Schen	1,000

Janitress.

Emma Johnson	300

Justices to the Police.

Thomas Murphy	1,800
Thomas H. Rochford	1,600
Wallace C. Hill	1,200

TELEPHONE NUMBERS CITY OFFICES.

Assessors—Seneca 1181.
Auditor—Seneca 532.
Board of Health—Seneca 80.
Bureau of Building—Seneca 246.
Bureau of Engineering—Seneca 510.
Bureau of Streets—Seneca 620.
Bureau of Water—Seneca 176-A.
City Chemist—Tupper 330.
City Clerk—Seneca 532.
Comptroller—Seneca 740.
Corporation Counsel—Seneca 650.
Department of Public Works—Seneca 1384.
Examiner of Engineers—Seneca 58.
Excise Department—Seneca 961.
Fire Department—Seneca 640.
Grade Crossing Commission—Seneca 1165.
Inspector of Steam Boilers—Seneca 58.
Mayor—Seneca 548.
Municipal Court—Seneca 429.
Overseer of the Poor—Seneca 906.
Park Commissioners—Seneca 1419.
Police Department—Seneca 514.
Superintendent of Education—Seneca 180.
Treasurer—Seneca 1430.

COMMON COUNCIL.

OFFICERS:

President Board of Aldermen.

   Jacob Kissinger $1,000

President Board of Councilmen.

   Christian Klinck.............   1,000

President Common Council.

   Chas. P. Woltz.   1,000

City Clerk.

   Mark S. Hubbell   2,500

Deputy City Clerk

   Charles F. Susdorf   2,000

BOARD OF ALDERMEN AND COMMON COUNCIL.

Sergeant-at-Arms.

   John Fraas, per session............ $3.00

Messenger.

Orvis Laurence, per session........ $1.75

BOARD OF COUNCILMEN.

Sergeant-at-Arms.

Nicholas Dwyer, per session....... 3.00

Messenger.

John Fraas, per session........... 1.75

ALDERMEN.

Twenty-five, each 1,000

COUNCILMEN.

Nine, each 1,000

Terms of office of following officers during pleasure of Mayor.

Clerk of the Markets.

Jacob M. Roesch................$1,800

Assistant Clerks of the Markets.

John Mock, Elk Street............ $900
Edward J. Toumey, Elk Street.... 800
Philip Klippel, Washington........ 900
Charles B. Umpleby, Washington.. 800
Julius Smith, Clinton Street....... 800
Anthony Stabenau, Broadway..... 900

Examiner of Stationary Engineers.

Fred C. Riester.................. 1,500

Inspector of Steam Boilers.

George Reil.. 1,500
(Term, three years.)

Assistant.

Henry Kumpf.................... 1,000

Inspector of Oils.

(Civil Service.)

Michael J. Noonan............... Fees

Harbor Master.

Robert C. Soper. 1,200
(Term, two years.)

Assistant.

John F. Eagan . . . . Honor

Bridge Tenders.

(Civil Service.)

Twelve, each $600

Poundkeeper.

(Civil Service.)

H. M. Wright 400

Keepers of Bathing Houses.

(Civil Service.)

M. J. Sullivan 300
John Foley 300

Keeper Public Bath House.

Cornelius O'Brien.

Matron.

Mrs. Mary O'Brien.

Keeper of Howard Cemetery.

Patrick Burke.

Official Printer.—1897.

The Wenborne-Sumner Co.

Official Paper.

The Buffalo Courier.

DEPARTMENT OF PARKS.

Commissioners.

His Honor, the Mayor, ex-officio.
Andrew Langdon.   John Guenther.
William S. Wicks.   Louis Zittel.
Norman W. Ransom.
Terms expire May 1, 1900.

Richard Hammond.   Charles R. Huntley.
John Hughes.   Nathan Wolff.
Robert M. Harding.
Terms expire May 1, 1902.

Bronson C. Rumsey. Britain Holmes.
David F. Day.   William Hengerer.
Ottomar Reinecke.
Term expires May 1, 1898.

OFFICERS.

William Hengerer, President.

Secretary and Treasurer.

George H. Selkirk $1,800

Superintendent.

William McMillan...........   3,000

Auditor and Paymaster.
J. L. Brothers..................$1,500
Botanical Director.
John F. Cowell.................. 1,600

STANDING COMMITTEES OF THE BOARD OF PARK COMMISSIONERS.

EXECUTIVE COMMITTEE.
William Hengerer, Chairman.
John Hughes.   Britain Holmes.
Andrew Langdon.   David F. Day.
            Robert M. Harding.

COMMITTEE ON GROUNDS AND ROADS.
Andrew Langdon.   John Hughes.
Bronson C. Rumsey.   David F. Day.
            Ottomar Reinecke.

COMMITTEE ON BUILDINGS.
Britain Holmes.   Norman W. Ransom.
William S. Wicks.   John Guenther.
            Richard Hammond.

AUDITING COMMITTEE.
John Hughes.   Andrew Langdon.
Nathan Wolff.   John Guenther.
            Charles R. Huntley.

COMMITTEE ON BOTANICAL AND ZOOLOGICAL COLLECTIONS.

David F. Day.   Robert M. Harding.
Ottomar Reinecke.   Nathan Wolff.
          Norman W. Ransom.

COMMITTEE ON MUSIC.

Robert M. Harding.   William S. Wicks.
          Louis Zittel.

COMMISSIONERS OF JURORS.

Willis H. Meads, Commissioner.
Henry H. Seymour, Dep. Commissioner.

CITY AND COUNTY HALL DEPARTMENT.

Trustees.
          Lyman M. Baker, Chairman.
Henry Breitwieser.   F. R. Whaley.
John G. Milburn.   Robert B. Foote.
          Henry V. Bisgood.

Secretary.
     Carl T. Chester $600

Superintendent.

W. F. Fisher, per year $2,000
Three Janitors and Floormen, each,
    per month. 60
One extra Janitor and Floorman,
    per month. 55
Three laborers, each, per month. . . 50

Engineers.

James M. Rowley, per year. 1,400
One Assistant, per year. 1,000
Two, Firemen, each, per month. . . . 55
One Watchman, per month. 65
Twenty-two Charwomen, each, per
    day 1
Two Elevator Conductors, each, per
    month 36
One Cabinet Repairer, per month. . 75

GRADE CROSSING COMMISSION.

R. B. Adam, Chairman.	W. J. Morgan.
F. Kendall.	A. F. Scheu.
E. H. Butler.	C. A. Sweet.
George Sandrock.	James Ryan.
H. D. Kirkover.	J. B. Weber.

CIVIL SERVICE COMMISSION OF THE CITY OF BUFFALO.

Charles B. Wheeler, Chairman.
William B. Dickinson, Secretary.
Florence M. Cowan, Stenographer.

Commissioners.

Eugene S. Simpson.
Chauncey P. Smith.
Chas. Mosier.
P. W. Van Peyma, M.D.
John Coleman.
Fred D. Lewis, M.D.
William F. Strasmer.
Charles B. Wheeler.
George A. Ricker.
Joseph B. Mayer.
John B. Olmstead.
Henry W. Sprague.
Henry C. Buswell, M.D.
George C. Fox.
W. D. Young, M.D.

Number of School Teachers on pay
    roll............................... 1,122
Number of Pupils registered at be-
    ginning of school year, Septem-
    ber, 1896....... 52,157

CITY OFFICIALS GIVING BONDS AND THE AMOUNTS THEREOF.

Comptroller $100,000
Deputy Comptroller................. 50,000
Auditor 5,000
Tax Sale Clerks, each............... 5,000
Treasurer 200,000
Deputy Treasurer................... 40,000
Receiving Teller.................... 20,000
Paying Tellers, Treasurer's office, each 20,000
Assessors, each 5,000
Corporation Counsel................. 5,000
Attorney 3,000
City Clerk. 5,000
Police Commissioners, each......... 5,000
Superintendent of Police........... 5,000
Assistant Superintendent of Police... 2,500
Clerk of Police.................... 5,000
Sealer of Weights and Measures...... 5,000
Assistant Sealers of Weights and
      Measures, each................. 5,000
Health Commissioner................ 5,000
Commissioners of Public Works, each 10,000
Cashier, Department of Public Works 10,000
Superintendent of Streets........... 5,000
Superintendent of Building......... 5,000

Water Superintendent	$10,000
Secretary and Treasurer Park Commissioners	10,000
Superintendent of Education	5,000
Overseer of the Poor	5,000
Deputy Overseer of the Poor	2,500
Police Justice	3,000
Justices of the Peace, each	2,000
Clerk of the Markets	10,000
Assistants at Markets, each	2,000
Harbor Master	1,000
Inspector of Steam Boilers	5,000
Examiner of Stationary Engineers	5,000

CITY MEMBERS OF THE BOARD OF SUPERVISORS.

TERMS EXPIRE JANUARY 1, 1898.

Ward	1	R	John A. Smith
"	2	D	William H. Ryan
"	3	R	Robert Gilkinson
"	4	D	John J. Collins
"	5	D	Thomas Scully
"	6	R	Frank Klipfel
"	7	R	Charles E. Dennstedt
"	8	R	Louis G. Roedel
"	9	D	George Hendler
"	10	R	William Darmstadter
"	11	D	Jacob Okoniewski
"	12	R	John Heintz
"	13	R	Martin Hasselbeck
"	14	R	Louis C. Dedo
"	15	R	George F. Aberth
"	16	R	Philip Erbes
"	17	R	George Ruel
"	18	R	Louis Zumstein
"	19	D	James D. Wilson
"	20	R	John Fisher
"	21	R	Charles Lanker
"	22	R	George F. Young
"	23	R	Neil McEachren
"	24	R	Thomas Tilson
"	25	R	Charles P. Brandel

THE POLICE CENSUS.

Taken by Precincts, by Patrolmen, after the Spring Exodus, in Three Days, and Reported to the Common Council May 6, 1895, Gave Buffalo a Population of 335,709.

The result of the enumeration by precincts is as follows:

Precinct No. 1, inhabitants	20,587
" " 2, "	23,192
" " 3, "	25,975
" " 4, "	36,238
" " 5, "	28,307
" " 6, "	31,478
" " 7, "	19,203
" " 8, "	63,654
" " 9, "	9,761
" " 10, "	23,362
" " 11, "	12,666
" " 12, "	29,633
" " 13, "	11,653
Total	335,709

Estimated number non-enumerated, because always absent from the city on Lake, Canal, Railway Contract and other work between May 1st and October 1st, families moving into the country for the summer, and others 20,000

Accretion 1895 to 1896 estimated .. 20,000

Grand Total 375,709

THE EXCISE COMMISSION.

APPOINTED UNDER CHAPTER 112 OF THE LAWS OF 1896, KNOWN AS THE RAINES LAW.

1. **Daniel O'Grady,** Special Deputy Comissioner of Excise for Erie County $2,000
2. Maurice F. Lindquist, Confidential Clerk........................... 1,500
3. Fred. O. Murray, Cashier....... 1,900
4. Andrew T. Kurtz, Assistant Cashier......................... 1,500
5. James F. Loftus, Auditor........ 1,300
6. George A. Woodward, Stenographer 1,200
7. Josiah S. McLaughlin, Bookkeeper 1,200
8. George E. Gaige 1,200

Specials Agents.

9. Jacob Pfanner 1,200
10. Robert W. Larkin................ 1,200

COUNTY OFFICIALS.

Terms of Office of Various Elective Positions in the City Government.

County Judge .... 6 years.
Surrogate 6   "
*Sheriff 3   "
*Coroner 3   "
*County Clerk..................... 3   "
*County Treasurer 3   "
*District Attorney................ 3   "
*Superintendent of Poor.......... 3   "
County Auditor.................... 4   "
Keeper of the Penitentiary........ 3   "
*Alms House Keeper............... 3   "
*Supreme Court Judge............14   "

The offices marked above by a star are those for which incumbents will be selected at the election of 1897, successful candidates taking their offices on January 1st, 1898.

CONSTABLES.

First Ward.................John Conway
Second Ward.................James Kane
Third Ward.............William H. Griven
Fourth Ward..............Frank J. Pinker
Fifth Ward.................James Moran
Sixth Ward.............Gurdon I. Ingersoll
Seventh Ward................Marcus Cohen
Eighth Ward.........Frederick Verstraaten
Ninth Ward..............Herman Geissler
Tenth Ward..............William Krangel
Eleventh Ward.......Lawrence T. Jamieson
Twelfth Ward..............George Scheter
Thirteenth Ward...........John M. Strabel
Fourteenth Ward......Henry J. Schwendler
Fifteenth Ward................W. A. Wilson
Sixteenth Ward.......Charles H. Handwerk
Seventeenth Ward..........Josiah Woodward
Eighteenth Ward...........Charles T. Linke
Nineteenth Ward............James Southard
Twentieth Ward..............Carl Anderson
Twenty-first Ward............Lorenzo Kent
Twenty-second Ward......William H. Craig
Twenty-third Ward....Robert H. Anderson
Twenty-fourth Ward.......Robert A. Locke
Twenty-fifth Ward.......George D. Feagles

LOCATION OF POLICE STATION HOUSES AND BOUNDARIES OF PRECINCTS.

No. 1—Corner Franklin and Seneca streets.

BOUNDARY.—South Michigan and Michigan street to Eagle, to Niagara, to Virginia, to the intersection of the south-westerly continuation of Virginia street and the westerly line of the State of New York, thence southeasterly along said line to its intersection with a continuation of the southerly line of South Michigan street.

No 2—403 Seneca street.

BOUNDARY.—Michigan street from Hamburg Canal to Clinton street, to Fillmore avenue, to Smith, to Perry, to Hamburgh, to Hamburgh Canal, to Michigan street.

No. 3—425 Pearl street.

BOUNDARY.—Niagara street from Eagle to Virginia, to Elmwood, to North, to Michigan, to Eagle, to Niagara street.

No. 4—Corner Sycamore and Ash streets.

BOUNDARY.—Michigan street, from Clinton to North, to Jefferson, to Clinton, to Michigan street.

No. 5—Corner Emily and Delavan avenue.

BOUNDARY.—Elmwood avenue from Utica street to Forest avenue, to Delaware, to centre line of Park Lake, along the centre line of Park Lake and Scajaquada Creek and the westerly continuation thereof to its intersection with the westerly line of the State of New York, along said State Line to its intersection with the westerly continuation of the centre line of Massachusetts street, along said line and Massachusetts street to Forest avenue to Rhode Island street, to Utica to Elmwood avenue.

No. 6—1444 Main street.

BOUNDARY.—North street from Elmwood to Jefferson street, to Best, to Roehrer, to Ferry, to Humboldt Parkway, to East Delavan, to City Line, to Delaware, to Forest, to Elmwood, to North.

No. 7—355 Louisiana street.

BOUNDARY.—Michigan and South Michigan streets to the Hamburgh Canal, to Hamburgh, to Perry, to Smith, to Buffalo Creek, to L. S. & M. S. R. R. tracks, to City Line, along said City Line and westerly extension thereof to its intersection with the south-westerly line of the State of New York, along said State

Line to its intersection with the southerly extension of the centre line of South Michigan street.

No. 8—484 William street.

BOUNDARY.—Clinton street from Jefferson to Babcock, to William, thence northerly to the "Y," following the "Y" and the Belt Line tracks to Sycamore, to Jefferson, to Clinton street.

No. 9 —Corner Seneca and Babcock streets.

BOUNDARY.—Clinton street from the City Line to Fillmore avenue, to Smith, to Buffalo River, to L. S. & M. S. R. R. tracks, to City Line, to Clinton street.

No. 10—566 Niagara street.

BOUNDARY.—Virginia from River Front to Elmwood, to Utica, to Rhode Island, to Front, to Massachusetts, to the westerly line of the State of New York, along said line to its intersection with a continuation of the westerly line of Virginia street.

No. 11—Corner Broadway and Bailey avenue.

BOUNDARY.—Clinton street City Line, to Babcock, to William, north to the "Y," along the "Y" and Belt Line to Sycamore, to Walden, to City Line, to Clinton street.

No. 12—1186 Genesee street.

BOUNDARY.—Walden avenue from City Line to Sycamore, to Jefferson, to Best, to Roehrer, to Ferry, to Humboldt Parkway, to East Delavan, to City Line, to Walden avenue.

No. 13—Corner Austin and Joslyn streets.

BOUNDARY.—Delaware avenue from the City Line to center line of Park Lake and Scajaquada Creek, to westerly line of State of New York, to westerly continuation of City Line. along City Line, to Delaware avenue.

WARD BOUNDARIES.

1st Ward.—Bounded by Exchange, Louisiana streets, Center line of Louisiana street extended, Lake Erie, Buffalo River and Main street.

2d Ward.—Bounded by Exchange, Red Jacket, Elk streets, Indian Reservation Line, Buffalo River and Louisiana street.

3d Ward.—Bounded by Eagle, Cedar, Swan, Spring streets, Myrtle avenue, Jefferson, Exchange and Main streets.

4th Ward.—Bounded by Eagle street, Fillmore avenue, Seneca street, Indian Reservation Line, Elk, Red Jacket, Exchange, Jefferson street, Myrtle avenue, Spring, Swan and Cedar streets.

5th Ward.—Bounded by Buffalo River, Indian Reservation Line, Seneca street, Fillmore Parkway, Clinton street, East City Line, South City Line, Lake Erie and Louisiana street extended.

6th Ward.—Bounded by Goodell, Michigan, Eagle and Main streets.

7th Ward.—Bounded by Broadway, Pratt, Eagle and Michigan streets.

8th Ward.—Bounded by Broadway, Adams, Eagle and Pratt streets.

9th Ward.—Bounded by Broadway, Fillmore Parkway, William and Adams streets.

10th Ward.—Bounded by William street, Fillmore avenue, Eagle and Adams streets.

11th Ward.—Bounded by Broadway, City Line, Clinton street and Fillmore avenue.

12th Ward.—Bounded by Genesee and Mortimer streets, Broadway and Michigan streets.

13th Ward,—Bounded by Genesee, Sherman, Broadway and Mortimer streets.

14th Ward.—Bounded by Sherman, Genesee streets, Walden avenue, City Line, and Broadway.

15th Ward.—Bounded by North, Mulberry, Goodell, Cherry, Hickory, Genesee, Michigan, Goodell and Main streets.

16th Ward.—Bounded by North, Jefferson, Genesee, Hickory, Cherry, Goodell and Mulberry streets.

17th Ward.—Bounded by Delavan avenue, Jefferson, North and Main streets.

18th Ward.—Bounded by Delavan avenue, City Line, Walden avenue, Genesee and Jefferson streets.

19th Ward.—Bounded by Porter and Front avenues, Court street, Terrace (east), Franklin street, Terrace, Main street, Buffalo River and Lake Erie.

20th Ward.—Bounded by Porter and Prospect avenues, Huron and Main streets, Terrace, Franklin street, Terrace (east), Court street, and Front avenue.

21st Ward.—Bounded by Hudson, Wadsworth streets, the Circle, North, Main, Huron streets and Prospect avenue.

22d Ward.—Bounded by Bird avenue, Grant, Hampshire, Sixteenth streets, Massachusetts, Fargo, Porter avenues and Niagara River.

23d Ward.—Bounded by Massachusetts avenue, the Circle, Richmond avenue, the Circle, Wadsworth and Hudson streets, Prospect, Porter and Fargo avenues.

24th Ward.—Bounded by Scajaquada Creek, Main and North streets, the Circle, Richmond avenue, the Circle, Massachusetts avenue, Sixteenth, Hampshire and Grant streets, Bird avenue, Black Rock Harbor, including Squaw Island.

25th Ward.—Bounded by Delavan avenue, Main street, Scajaquada Creek, Black Rock Harbor, Niagara River, City Line, Town Line Road and City Line, including Strawberry Island.

TAXABLE VALUATION BY WARDS.

Ward	Valuation
1	$18,665,185
2	3,338,165
3	18,004,660
4	4,315,745
5	11,795,335
6	13,028,815
7	3,419,180
8	3,220,290
9	2,860,920
10	2,684,300
11	9,301,060
12	2,405,915
13	2,197,820
14	6,607,285
15	4,760,035
16	2,094,550
17	6,997,895
18	11,304,795
19	10,322,325
20	22,460,085
21	17,712,025
22	8,456,125
23	7,840,300
24	27,051,720
25	18,327,865
Total	$239,172,345

TOTAL VOTE BY WARDS.

Predicated on vote cast for Governor, Nov. 3d, 1896.

Ward		
Ward	1	1,359
"	2	1,901
"	3	2,622
"	4	2,299
"	5	2,773
"	6	1,758
"	7	2,033
"	8	1,961
"	9	2,260
"	10	1,507
"	11	3,565
"	12	1,657
"	13	1,804
"	14	3,490
"	15	1,962
"	16	1,717
"	17	3,546
"	18	4,228
"	19	2,074
"	20	2,138
"	21	2,962
"	22	3,035
"	23	2,800
"	24	4,202
"	25	3,007
Total		62,660

VOTERS BY WARDS.

Registration of electors in the city of Buffalo, year 1891 to 1896, inclusive.

Ward	1891	1892	1893	1894	1895	1896
1	1671	1678	2525	1715	1567	1565
2	1810	2010	1830	2074	1867	2039
3	2687	3174	2764	3030	2386	2873
4	2143	2472	2190	2426	2159	2448
5	1863	2262	2187	2610	2370	2944
6	1881	2044	1869	1938	1665	1900
7	1978	2177	2056	2141	1984	2157
8	1795	1971	1868	1997	1864	2053
9	1894	2210	2105	2291	2105	2349
10	1314	1430	1452	1575	1403	1479
11	2043	2751	2718	3230	2917	3590
12	1602	1742	1693	1725	1665	1748
13	1635	1827	1674	1826	1610	1883
14	1888	2660	2622	3168	2965	3666
15	1823	2027	1910	1961	1896	2053
16	1551	1715	1622	1752	1632	1798
17	2323	2889	2904	3215	3149	3703
18	2439	3213	3215	3759	3659	4452
19	2144	2450	2317	2577	2084	2188
20	2047	2279	2096	2304	1965	2249
21	2651	2833	2788	2903	2646	3090
22	2230	2643	2652	2859	2746	3316
23	2318	2610	2557	2730	2527	2882
24	2497	2950	3143	3561	3525	4368
25	2042	2481	2539	2904	2658	3169
	50273	58498	57296	62271	57014	65962

APPOINTIVE OFFICERS AND TERMS OF OFFICE.

OFFICE.	BY WHOM APPOINTED.	TERM OF OFFICE.
Coms. of Pub. Wks (2)	Mayor..........	4 years.
Chief Engineer.......	Comrs. of Pub Works.	During pleasure of Board.
Water Supt	"	"
Supt. of Building. ..	"	"
City Clerk	Com. Council..	1 year.
Fire Comrs. (3).......	Mayor	6 years.
Clerk of Markets.....	"	During pleasure of Mayor.
Asst. Clerk of Markets	"	"
Police Comrs. (2). ..	"	6 years.
Sealer of Weights and Measures.	Board of Police	1 year.
Harbor Master	Mayor..........	2 years.
Oil Inspector.	"	During term of Mayor appointing him.
Examr. of Stationary Engineers.	"	Until his successor is appointed.
Inspector of Steam Boilers.	"	3 years, unless sooner removed for cause.
Exam. and Super. Bd. of Plumbers and Plumbing.	"	3 years. See Chap. 602, Laws of 1892.
Auditor	Comptroller....	By and with the advice and consent of Com. Council.
Health Commissioner	Mayor..........	5 years.
School Examiners (5)	"	5 years.
Bridge Tenders.......	"	Civil Service.
Keeper of Howard Cemetery.	"	During pleasure of Mayor.
Kpr. Bath. Houses (4)	"	"
Park Comrs. (15).....	"	6 years.
Pound Keeper........	"	Civil Service.
Civil Ser. Comrs. (15)	"	During pleasure of Mayor.
City and County Hall Trustees (6).	Appel. Div. of Sup. Court.	6 years.
Comr. of Jurors.	Judges of Sup. and Co. Court	3 years.

THE LOW TAX RATE OF 1897.

Property Owners of the City of Buffalo, with Added Advantages, Pay Less Taxes than in Years Preceding.

The following figures, given out by the Assessors early in May, show that the tax rate of 1897 will be $14.1788 per thousand dollars of valuation, as against $15.0160 per thousand in 1896, and $15.3956 in 1895, showing a steady ratio of decrease of the burden of taxation upon holders of real estate.

The following tabulated statement shows the growth in property valuation for ten years and the tax rate for each year of the decade:

Year.	Increase of Valuation.	Tax-rate.
1888	$4,439,350	$14.3638
1889	24,433,135	14.14646
1890	4,855,610	14.68217
1891	17,598,070	15.814837
1892	17,127,320	15.169182
1893	25,488,105	15.843121
1894	7,553,520	15.332054
1895	4,524,995	15.396
1896	4,320,945	15.016059
1897	8,415,930	14.178799

This, without the lamp tax, which this year adds .7473 per thousand, making the total rate of general taxation $14.92 per thousand.

The amount to be raised by taxation this year is $3,507,668.67.

TURNING AWAY CONVENTIONS.

Buffalo Has More Prospective Guests Than She Can Accommodate In 1897.

A glance at the chapter on ''Conventions Past and Present'' will reveal an apparent falling off in the number of organizations which are scheduled to meet in Buffalo during the present year, but there is an excellent reason for this, which is, that the Mayor has been compelled in many instances to decline the honor for the city of entertaining all those who have desired to hold their annual meetings in Buffalo. Already arrangements have been made for the accommodation of enough great conclaves of fraternal and other organizations to make every week during July and August convention week this summer.

Buffalo has the coolest summer climate of any city in the country, as will be found proven in a table of comparative weather statistics, officially vouched for, on another page.

INDEX.

A

B

PAGE.

W